Ascending The Hill…
With a Bossy Dog

The Continued Adventures of a Worshiping Mom
Book 2

Nicki Harris

ISBN: **1979783586**
ISBN-13: **978-1979783583**

DEDICATION

To my wonderful loves. You make everything I do, and all the hell I go through, worth it. Your smiles, laughter, very great patience, and your belief in me is literally the wings beneath my wings…As cheesy as that sounds. So at the risk of diving even deeper into cheesiness, it is with a sincere heart that I dedicate this book to my precious family.

CONTENTS

Nicki Harris

FOREWORD

Wow. A series. I never even thought I would write ONE book, and here I am publishing a SECOND. WHAT?! I'm not sure if you're just hopping onto this craziness that I call a series, or if you've braved the insanity of my first book , "Hidden Treasure, Mysteries, & Sea Monsters", but I hope that you find hope and grace in every line. I hope that you are encouraged by my failures and by my victories…But mostly, I hope that you feel the warm love a Father God who really does think you're amazing and who really is your biggest fan. You were made for love. Inhale that truth for a second and then if you are a brave soul, lol…Dive into the continued adventures of a worshiping mama

Holy Gossip

Gossip.

A word that can describe the single-handed destruction of one's character.

Gossip.

A word that causes every leader in a house of faith to cringe as if Freddy Krueger had just had his way with a chalkboard.

Gossip.

Something that no passionate believer would ever admit to being a willing party to.

And yet....

I bet you think you know where I'm going with this, huh?

A rant about an epidemic of rot in the Bride of Christ where we deface each other?

A couple of choice scriptures to quote that supremely make my point?

Well, nope.

I'm not talking about gossip as it applies to each other...I'm talking about gossip as it applies to our God.

**Yep...I'm talking about gossiping about the
 Creator of the Universe.**

Hahaha. Papa just told me that some of you might even think you know where THIS is going...that I'm putting a positive spin on it...like telling the world about Him is the 'gossip' I'm referring to.

Not so.

At all.

I'm talking about straight up, bold face, gossip.

Got your attention?

Lol, let me explain:

Thursday morning I was stealing a little time with my Lover and was lost in the song "He's Like" [1] that Steffany Frizzell Gretzinger sings. She was pouring out these characteristics of our Abba: "He's like wind, He's like the rain, He's like fire, He's like oil.."

And it was so powerful.

You could feel the depth of her passion for Him and the deep conviction with which she sang those simple identifying lyrics. You could tell from her body language, her facial expression, her devotion, that she not only believed this about Him, but that she KNEW it.

Some of us have had this awesome, humbling honor of being in His presence when He blew across us like wind, fell upon us and cleansed us like the rain, burned us with His fiery passion, soothed and healed us like oil...Not in theory, but in REALITY.

Oh, to know Him this way...

Even had I not already made my own history with Him, just seeing her unabashedly adore this God would have made me believe it. There is just something powerful in first hand knowledge.

I was listening to the crowd singing and worshiping with her…I, myself, was caught up in it with her.

And then God spoke:

"Second-hand knowledge"

I was a tad startled...I mean, how random is that? Like, really..?

"Second-hand knowledge?"

"Yes," He replied.

I waited for more, but He didn't go any further. I love/hate when He does that, hahaha. It's like He gives me just enough to peak my interest so I will dig to find Him and the revelation He has waiting for me.

So I sat.

Thinking.

"Second-hand knowledge.....second-hand knowledge....What IS second-hand knowledge??"

So I looked it up.(Thanks dictionary.com!)

"*2***sec ond hand**

[sek-uh-nd-hand]
adjective
not directly known or experienced; obtained from others or from books: Most of our knowledge is secondhand."

My revelation sensors started tingling, lol.
Why was Steffany's worship so powerful? Why were Bill Johnson's, Heidi Baker's, Apostle Ron Carpenter's words so life changing?

It was all....

"*3***first hand**

[furst-hand]
adverb
from the first or original source: We heard the news of the accident firsthand from a witness.
adjective
direct from the source: firsthand knowledge of the riot."

Could it be that the reason our houses of faith are lacking in the miraculous...Lacking in the setting of captives free...Lacking in the tangible manifest is because we, as leaders, have grown lazy in our chase of the Holy One...That we have settled for second hand information because it sounds like Him, instead of seeking Him out daily and spending time with Him to get to know Him so we can say what He is truly like...As if ANY mortal could ever truly know who He is?

Is it bad to repeat stories of the goodness, faithfulness, miracles, and judgments of God?

NO! Absolutely NOT!

In fact that's biblical! He warned the Israelites against NOT telling the future generations about it, but what I'm hitting at is the longer you retell without experiencing it yourself, the more opportunity there is for twisting and polluting the character of God, Himself.

Our testimony of His nature and His heart will not come back void...The Word of God says this clearly, but think about this, if you will.

Which is more compelling in a court of law? A firsthand or secondhand witness?

Along the same lines, which is more compelling in a setting of faith? A firsthand knowledge of the heart of Abba Father, or secondhand information that we have 'heard' to be true?

It's obvious when the two are compared side by side...**Why can't WE see it?**

Papa...We want to know You more...I want to know You more. I want what comes out of my mouth in worship, in word, in scolding my children, in ministering to my husband, in teaching, in the grocery store, in the hospital, in the parking lot...in my LIFE to be FIRST hand knowledge.

I live to know You more.

ENDNOTES:

1 - He Is Like : Written by Tim Cone and Joy Maves, © Copyright Forerunner Music 2008
2 - Definition of 'second hand' from www.dictionary.com
3 - Definition of "first hand" from www.dictionary.com

The Bloody Sheet

So...With our youth purity conference coming up, I've really been thinking a lot about "purity" as a topic. Thinking a lot about how I can possibly come at this in a way that hasn't been dragged thru the proverbial gauntlet of religious ka-ka SO many times that it's absolutely wretched to this generation...and everyone else...so much so that teens avoid anything labeled "purity" and churches are afraid to touch it with a ten foot pole.

I mean, this generation needs the message of sexual purity...For their LIVES sakes, these days...But you almost have to TRICK them with a gimmick or a NON purity related theme to get them to even THINK about coming to a seminar or conference talking about it.

Then it dawned on me.

What do we normally cram down their throats at theses well-meaning conferences? Granted, I've been at a couple really awesome ones. Totally not talking about those, so cool your jets. I'm speaking generally...Broadly...About the church in America as a whole.

Our usual 'purity' talks usually consist of a list of rules that girls and guys must follow to be pure. Do's and don'ts, if you will, that if they follow them, they will be seen as 'pure' and ultimately will meet their prince or princess charming and all will be well.

In short? We set them up for failure and condemnation.

Now, before you start hurling your religiously indignant spears, let me clarify.

We can all agree that one can live 'physically' pure and still be completely and totally IM-pure. Just because we teach them how to NOT be counted among the whores and man-whores, doesn't mean that their minds don't go there and dwell there.

Our slap on their 'physical' hands and all the statistics that we scare them to death with won't be in the front of her mind and heart when Daddy has abandoned her and Brandon is telling her that he loves her and will always be there for her...in the back of his car.

Look at the teen and college age pregnancy rate these days. Look at the statistics of STDs that are spreading. Look at the abortion rates among teens and college age young women. Even scarier? Look at the cases of cervical cancer in young women these days...staggering.

Obviously what we are 'teaching' them isn't working.

Want to know why?

Because we have been teaching them an upside down truth.

We are telling them to act pure, when they don't even understand what purity really is...Heck...most of us don't even know what it really is. We automatically attach a sexual label to it when, in reality, purity is by definition:

*1***pu·ri·ty**

/ˈpyoȯritē/

Noun
    1.   Freedom from contamination.

*2***pure**

/pyoȯr/

Adjective
    1.   Not mixed or adulterated with any other substance or material.

Now hear my heart in this, sexual purity is a vital aspect of a believer's life, but unless we address the REAL purity issue...Physical, mental, emotional purity will always be a struggle and an open door for the enemy to enter with condemnation and guilt...and destruction. Honestly, I think its been his plan all along...To distort the sex issue and the teaching of purity from the beginning. He attaches shame to it and God created sex to a BLESSING not the shameful thing that the church has turned it into.

In the Jewish culture, purity was celebrated. Weddings were family affairs and after the vows, there was no celebration until the marriage was consummated and the bloody sheet was thrown over the door. The blood on the sheet was proof that the bride was pure and at that point the celebration began in full swing, celebrating the union.

Haha, imagine being a kid at that party..."Oh no...Did they get in a fight??" HA!

But my point is that it was a culture of purity. I imagine that sheet opened opportunities for conversations wedding after wedding, and so sexual purity was just...Normal...Expected...Celebrated.

Yeah.

Not so much in this culture.

Why is sexual purity such a problem, now?

You know, I think back on the times in my life when I really struggled with it, myself, and I asked myself why it was so hard for me then, versus now.

Then, maybe it was Abba, maybe it was just personal revelation...Either way, I realized that I had no IDEA what real purity was.

"Yes, actually, I did..." I argued with my own revelation, "I went to the conferences...Like a 'good girl'. I mean, c'mon! I listened and took it all in. I was seriously fervent when I dedicated myself to purity, but it didn't seem to stick when I was "in the moment" even into the earlier years of my marriage.

Then, as I sat pondering all this, I realized that I knew exactly what sexual purity was, but REAL purity...the kind that stops all thoughts and temptations that are not beneficial or pure from becoming reality...I had no CLUE what that looked like. That's why I was constantly struggling with "purity" and constantly feeling like a failure and a disappointment to my God.

So I've been thinking.

Scary, right?

Where does sexual purity COME from? Then I was reminded of my relationship with my husband and a time when I almost made a terrible mistake in regard to the purity of our relationship. I thought about what was happening in our relationship at that moment in time that would even make me vulnerable to be tempted like that.

When we first married...Oh...There was no way...No WAY anybody could ever catch my eye. I was SO in love and it was so EASY to be just his. I never even dreamed about doing anything that would hurt him...And if I was tempted, it got shut down immediately because I LOVED him so much it hurt and I couldn't destroy his heart, his trust in me, or what we had. He was everything to me second to God alone.

Then about 5 years into our marriage, he was working nights and I was working days at a nameless restaurant that specializes in wings and beautiful women in orange shorts. We never saw each other and when we did, it was in passing or he was sleeping. There was no real communication, no physical touch, no dates, no intimacy (feeling close)....Just...The reality that we were married, but we lived separate lives.

Was I intentional about connecting with Him? No. I totally laid every bit of that responsibility on him. Had I been more intentional with connecting with him, I would've never even been tempted. But my lack of connection with his heart, caused me to waver in my own feelings toward my covenant with him...I was bombarded everyday with attention, adoration, and others opinions (who were not married and had no respect for our covenant) about what I should do and who I should be...And because I was not secure in my own identity or relationship with my husband, I almost made a grave mistake.

See, our relationship with God is the same. At first, we are SO in love and there isn't much that we can be tempted with, but as time goes by, we lose that 'connected' feeling with Him and suddenly those things that weren't tempting before become more appealing...Especially when there are those in your life who have little or no respect for your relationship with Him and are constantly feeding you lies about who you SHOULD be as opposed to who He says you are....

Which is His.

It is in those dangerous places that we find our sexual purity being tested and we find ourselves falling into sexual death. We aren't 'in love' any more and so we aren't as concerned about hurting Him...Or at least we don't think we are until it happens.

I think about where I am now with Christ as opposed to then, and I think about how things come at me left and right. Its inevitable that I'm going to get hit hard, what with the platform that He has placed me on, but you know something? I'm not even tempted that much anymore...You know why?

It's so easy to obey when you're in love.

I filter every decision I make through Him...Will this hurt

my Beloved? Will this damage the intimacy that we share? Will this affect the sweetness of His presence when I enter in...The precious way He draws near even when I don't ask him to? If the answer to ANY of those is "yes", then my answer is a resounding "NO."

Why?

Because "You are not defined by the temptations you resist, you are defined by the virtues you embrace."[3]

I want this generation to be the ones who see His face and the word says this,

"Who may ascend the mountain of the Lord? Who may stand in His holy place? He who has clean hands and a pure heart, who does not lift up his soul to an idol or swear by what is false. He will receive blessing from the Lord and vindication from God his Savior. Such is the generation of those who seek Him, who seek Your face, O God of Jacob." Ps 24:3-6[4]

If we are in love…If our hearts are pure...If we are in an intimate relationship with Him, our sexual purity will be an overflow of our relationship with Him. It happens naturally.

Maybe if teaching sexual purity isn't working...And newsflash...It isn't… Maybe, just maybe, we should be teaching about falling in Love with Him...About having a relationship with Him and then teen pregnancies just might not be an issue anymore...STDs just might not be an issue anymore...AIDS could possibly no longer be the threat that it is...Young women wouldn't be dying of cervical cancer...Couples would be able to have children instead of dealing with sterility because of decisions made years before in the heat of the moment..

It's so easy to say "no" when you are in love...

ENDNOTES:

1 – Definition of purity from www.dictionary.com
2 – Definition of pure from www.dictionary.com
3 – Quote from Kris Vallotton
4 – Palm 24:3-6 Holy Bible, New International Version®, NIV® Copyright © 1973, 1978, 1984, 2011 by Biblica, Inc.®

So, Exactly What IS Worship??

So, recently someone asked me to write a 500-word essay describing what worship is and how to flesh it out.

Easy, right?

Yeah, I thought so too.

Ehhhhnotsomuch.

The topic wasn't the hard part. It was the 500-word part.

I mean, worship is so much more than ANY of us can EVER hope to confine within a literary work.

SO! I asked Abba to help me write this thing, mainly because if He doesn't help, it stinks.

Haha.

Don't judge. It's true, lol.

Anywho, I had a revelation in the midst of this essay and I

wanted to share it with you.

So here is the 536-word essay...hey, I tried to keep it at 500...

Enjoy. :)

"That moment. You know what I'm talking about. That epic moment when imagination meets reality and it exceeds everything you thought it could possibly be. That moment when your soul is moved so deeply that all you can do is close your eyes and soak in that moment, relish the moment, love the moment, because to do anything else would seem...a travesty. In that moment...you worship. The best example I can think of is when I stood in the solitary valley of an Alaskan mountain range for the very first time. I had seen pictures and knew it was a beautiful place. I had even heard people talk about how breathtaking it was, and I was convinced! I believed them! But I had never seen it, experienced it for myself. There I stood, in the presence of pure, unadulterated, unfiltered, untouched, uninhabited majesty and I was...breathless. Even though I had heard stories of this, it could never do justice to the reality. My imagination had done such an injustice to this moment that, when the reality met my imagination, all I could do was weep...Completely overtaken with awe and wonder...And my first response, the automatic, knee-jerk response was adoration and reverence...in other words, worship. No one had to tell me to be in awe. No one had to tell me to respond. Why? Because it's what we are wired to do. Naturally.

Some of us, like me and my Alaskan mountains, have seen beautiful worship and worshipers. Some of us have even been told how breathtaking worship can be, but it's not until we actually step into that valley for ourselves and open our eyes to all that it can be, that we actually experience the wonder of who God is and who we are not, and who we ARE...and our automatic, knee-jerk response is worship. We do it naturally. Not because someone sings a certain song. Not because someone says, "Raise your hands and worship!", but because we, ourselves have willingly stepped into the pure, unadulterated, unfiltered, untouched, uninhibited presence of a mighty God and our imagination meets reality. It's in that moment that we realize how very much more He is than we ever could've imagined and we are undone.

I've often gone back to that moment in Alaska. I wondered why it moved me so much and then I realized that those glorious mountains were doing exactly what they were made to do! The bible says that the "mountains will burst into song before you"[1] and "burst into singing, you mountains, you forests and all your trees,"[2] and, even though it was silent, those mountains were singing. They were singing and, because they were settled in their purpose, it caused my purpose to rise up, too. It caused this feeling of intense love and adoration to rise up. It caused me to worship. When we realize who we are, when we discover our purpose and begin to settle into it, that's the purest form of worship! Being who you were created to be is worship! And it will cause others' purposes to rise up, too. It will compel others to worship, too! Come! Let's worship together!"

ENDNOTES:

*1 – Isaiah 55:12 Holy Bible, New International Version®, NIV® Copyright © 1973, 1978, 1984, 2011 by **Biblica, Inc.**®*
*2 – Isaiah 44:23 Holy Bible, New International Version®, NIV® Copyright © 1973, 1978, 1984, 2011 by **Biblica, Inc.**®*

Not The Brightest Light In The Tool Shed

So I had a moment.

I recently attended a school of healing ministry and during a moment when I probably should've been paying closer attention, I was off in my little happy place just...soaking... in the tangible Presence. In a ballroom filled with almost 1000 perfectly good, relatively comfy chairs, I had found myself a nice, secluded, little corner and had parked my hind parts unceremoniously on the floor.

If I could've disappeared completely, I would have.

Bridget (my fellow sojourner in this particular education in the areas of effective flakiness), later laughed and said that she looked over during worship and noticed that she couldn't see me anymore...And then I just appeared from behind the heavy wall curtain that the hotel staff had pushed back into my corner.

Haha. Yep.

I love people...Like I LOVEEEEE people....

But I don't like people.

Don't like crowds. Don't like to socialize.

Makes me nervous...And edgy.

Give me solitude any day.

AnyWHO!

I was somewhere between listening and dreaming, when Papa startled me with:

"Look at the chandelier."

I opened my eyes and glanced up at the massive crystal creation suspended over the heads of about fifty of us.

"Ok. I'm looking at it…" His request just didn't compute...So I must admit that when I looked up at that hulking collection of glass, that I was a tad bit of a brat.

Just a tad.

Thankfully He is NOT me and is ultimately patient.

"What do you see?" He asked me.

I was now REALLY looking at this thing....Trying to figure out what He wanted me to see or to say....But all I saw was,

"Crystals...and light. I see...points..?"

I was trying to notice anything and everything that could be of significance.

"I see the support and the extension rod...?" (Which at that moment, I decided that it was very skinny and not quite big enough to satisfy my being okay with sitting under that thing....Thankfully I wasn't.)

I finally concluded with, "It's pretty."

I could almost hear the *"mhm...now you're getting it"* and the swish as He nodded His head.

"So are My people. They are pretty, but they, like this chandelier are an artificial light source...and they are symmetrically perfect."

I looked at this chandelier again with newfound interest.

"And they are dusty." He continued.

"Hmm…"

"From lack of movement."

My heart constricted with His words.

"They are too perfect to move...and quite expensive. If they move around too much, their thin support system would not bear up under the weight of their perfection and they would fall to the ground and everything that

makes them beautiful would shatter....And so they sit. Perfect, dusty, content to be an object of admiration."

What could I say to that?? I had been guilty of that too!!

OHDEARGOD!

Tears began to slip out of the corners of my eyes as I gazed fixatedly upon that chandelier...I'm sure people who happened to take notice probably thought I was a little strange...Sitting in the corner...Rocking back and forth...Gazing up into a chandelier...Crying and repenting...

Wait.

I was at a conference with people flakier than me.

 Scratch that, lol.

"They are useless outside of the church," He continued. *"They have no power in the world. My lost sheep have no use for pretty, hanging objects of beauty that provide no warmth."*

By this time, I was dutifully convicted, wrecked, and just short of a full on ugly-cry. I prepared myself for His next words. I repented before He could even speak it. I almost wailed out loud, my guilt and my fervent promise to get off my pedestal...To detach myself from the artificial source and connect to the real Flame. I promised to bring warmth to the lost and hopeless....

Again...had I not been at this particular conference...People...Well, they would be sure that I had backslidden and was coming back home.

But no amount of snottin' and repentin' could have prepared my heart for the destruction that was coming when He actually spoke.

In the middle of my almost hysterical internal rant, He said, *"You are not one of these..."*

"And Papa, I PROMISE that I will do better.." sniff, cough, sniff, sniff. "Wait...what?...."

"You, daughter, are a candle with a real flame that can not be extinguished..."

My body began to tremble as much as my lips were.

"...You are a light that I have ignited and one that I will use to ignite others who will break the back of the powers of darkness. You will bring peace, comfort, joy, warmth, and child-like belief and faith."

I gulped for air as the reality of His precious praise washed over me. The God of all creation was praising ME. Who am I?? WHO. AM. I. That He would honor ME with HIS praise..??

I was definitely not the brightest light in the toolshed by any means, but BY GOD! I was a light!! And my Papa said I was REAL!!

It was time for full on ugly cry.

And I didn't even care.

The Victor's Crown

HOLY. MERCY. COW.

So today (while I was packing for my trip to NC) I was listening to a song that Kristan and I will be practicing tonight with our amazing worship team.

I was listening to this and working, singing lightly with my mouth and my mind while my hands were busy sorting laundry, starting more, and deciding which outfits to take with. I've been sick for a while, so it's hard to REALLY sing. Not super sick, but for a week I was just...Gross...And now for another week my body has still been recovering. My lungs have taken the hardest hit. It probably would be a little better if I wasn't such a fool about incense...

ANYWHO.

Amidst all the "busy work" I found myself becoming engrossed in the dynamically thematic elements of this song...I mean...This song is SO stinkin' theatrical and so expertly done...You just can't help but be drawn in.

So! I decided that this type of song merited a little more than the cursory "practice" and I set my work down and proceeded to engross myself in identifying with the message AND the melody.

I started the song over and closed my eyes and lifted my face and hands heavenward.

I stepped up to the boom stand in front of the sink in the great auditorium that is my kitchen and allowed the score to wash over my spirit as I eagerly anticipated the forthcoming lyrical.

I could feel the warmth of the stage lights on my skin (the sun streaming thru the kitchen window over a sink full of dishes that needed my attention).

The crowd was waiting in excited expectation as the strings quieted.

I opened my mouth:

[1]"You are always fighting for us. Heaven's angels all around..." My spirit shook. Apparently, I had some company in the room.

"My delight is found in knowing, that You wear the Victor's crown.

You're my help and my defender, You're my Savior and my Friend..." Ninja tears assaulted my eyes.

"By Your grace I live and breathe to worship You..." My lungs began to hurt.

"At the mention of Your greatness, in Your name I will bow down...In Your presence fear is silenced, for You wear the Victor's crown.

Let Your glory fill this temple..." I could feel the tremble start at my feet....

Fill this temple...Fill this temple...Fill THIS temple...I am the temple of the Living God...Fill THIS temple!

"Let Your power overflow"...Yes!!

"By Your grace I live and breathe to worship You.." My lungs spasmed and I coughed deeply, painfully.

"Halleluuuuuuuuu-jah, You have overcome, You have overcome!"

Yes!! Jesus! You have overcome!

"Halleluuuuuuuuu-jah!! Jesus, You have overcome the wooooooooorrrrrrrrld!"

I twirled out of the kitchen/auditorium and flitted across the nation of my dining room and into the world arena of my living room. The crowd there was MUCH larger and His presence was electric as I began the next verse:

"You are ever interceding as the lost become the found, You can never be defeated for You wear the Victor's crown..."

WOO!

"Look at Me." He commanded.

I whirled around immediately and fixed my eyes on the Lion

painting above my French doors.

Haha, like I flipped around so fast my glasses almost came flying off.

"Sing to Me." He commanded.

"You are Jesus, the Messiah. You're the hope of all the world,"

No longer was I there with nations.

I was present with the Lamb of God...The Lion of the tribe of Judah.

"By Your grace I live and breathe to worship You...!!"

My lungs seized. I coughed and coughed and coughed and gagged and coughed, but I couldn't stop singing. I just couldn't stop breathing. I had to breathe. My worship flew on the wings of my breath and I HAD to worship, so I HAD to breathe. I live and BREATHE to worship Him! There was no way, in the thickness of His glorious presence, there in my living room, that I was going to crap out.

He is too worthy.

He is too wonderful.

He is too HOLY.

"Hallelu--(COUGH!)-hoo-(COUGH!)-HEEYAH!(COUGH! COUGH! Gag)"

My eyes were fixed upon the golden eyes of the Lion above me...

(and before you get all crazy religious on me, no I most certainly do NOT believe that painting is Jesus...BUT!! He DID tell me to paint it as a reminder of Who is always watching over our family and our purpose...So in essence...It's a representation of Him...Say what you will. Join in with those who call me a "flake". I just do not care. I'm madly in love with Him and He speaks to me...Touches me...Impregnates me with His glory...And...Well. You get the idea…End rant.)

"You have OVER-(COUGH), You have OVER-(COUGH)..."

DANG IT!! LUNGS!! YOU WILL RECEIVE OXYGEN!! BRONCHIAL TUBES YOU WILL RELAX!!

"Halleluuuuuuuuuu-YAH!! (COUGH), JE-(COUGH), You have OVERCO-(COUGH) the WORLD!!!(COUGH! COUGH! Gag, COUGH!)

I was sweating from the effort by this time but I refused to let this ridiculous coughing fit prevent me from expressing my worship with everything I had in me. As long as I had breath, I was GOING to make a sound...

Dang it!

As I continued to look into the eyes of that painting, it was like the flames on the right side of it began to come to life. They began swirling and extending further out past the canvas.

And then...

He shook His glorious, fiery, windswept, mane....And I gasped.

And coughed.

Y'all, I saw that painting morph and a full bodied Lion of fire stepped off of the canvas and into the atmosphere of my living room.

"EVERY HIGH THING MUST COME DOWN!
(COUGH, COUGH, COUGH)
EVERY STRONGHOLD SHALL BE
(COUGH)BROKEN!
YOU WEAR THE VICTOR'S CROWN! (COUGH, COUGH)
YOU WILL (COUGH)-VERCOME, YOU WILL OVER-(COUGH)!"

My body started rejoicing. Like leaping and spinning wildly...

Yep.

Right there in my living room.

Slam-dancing with the Holy One of Israel in a most undignified fashion.

Throwing myself into the air, falling on my butt, picking myself up, spinning and jumping and coughing and gagging and yelling until the song finished and I collapsed, exhausted, sweating, coughing my lungs up, and thoroughly spent on my back on the floor in front of my fireplace.

And then...

He settled in...So heavy...So gentle...Ohhhh...The kabod...

Kabod: The weighty importance and shining majesty which accompany God's presence. The basic meaning of the Hebrew word kabod is heavy in weight.2

I tried to lift my outstretched arms...Even just to roll over, but the weight was too much...

So I laid there...As the song that I had on repeat, began again.

"Thank you, Jesus....", tears began to slip from the corners of my eyes and I could do nothing to wipe them. I couldn't move ANYTHING.

"I love you, Jesus..."

"Shhhhhhhh.....Beloved One....shhhhh...."

I shushed.

"I want to show you something..." He whispered.

"Okay..."

I laid there, paralyzed, eyes closed…And I began to see images...In the negative...Like a film negative...You know, the reversed colors. First it was smoke...And then the smoke swirled and formed eyes...Large, intense, Lion-esk eyes that swirled and curled and then the smoke swirled again and the eyes became like eagle eyes...Just as intense...

Then the smoke blew away and there was a circular swirl that reminded me of a violent ocean wave crashing...Only it was in a continuous circle (kind of like the buffering circle on when a program is loading), crashing and then growing, then crashing, then growing.

Then the smoke blew away again and it was like gentle waters washing up on the shore over and over again.

Then it was gone.

I tested my arms and the weight had lifted.

"Halleluuuu-yah...You have overcome, You have overcome..." was playing in my ear buds.

I rolled over and shakily got to my hands and knees.

"Well...I have NO idea what that all meant, Jesus," I whispered weakly, "but, I don't have to. Thank You for sharing your secrets with me...I know that You will make it clear soon…" Those sneaky ninja tears attacked my eyes again.

And then the Son of God sang to me.

"Halleluuuu-yah. You have overcome. You will overcome.
Halleluuuu-yah, Nicki, you have overcome the world.
Every high thing must come down. Every stronghold shall be broken.
You wear the Victor's crown. You have overcome, you will overcome."

Annnnnnd I was in the floor again.

Too much, Jesus....You love me too much....

ENDNOTES:

1 – The Victor's Crown written by Darlene Zschech, Israel Houghton, and Kari Jobe ©Integrity Music 2013
2 – Definition for kabod from www.dictionary.com

Well, Well, Tattle-Tale...

Here's the deal.

I'm a chicken.

A great big colossal chicken.

And Papa knows it.

Mainly, because He's, well, GOD... But also because I have told Him MANY times how hard of a time I've been having with teaching the series on healing that we are doing with our students this month. I've only shared that with a VERY few trusted people who I know will cover and pray for me.

Every second and fourth Tuesday nights I attend a ladies home group that is...Well...No words can describe the levels of glory that we splash around in, there.

This past week me, a friend, one of our students, and one of our youth sponsors got there late. As we walked in, we walked right slam into the presence of the King.

One of the ladies was dancing in the middle of the circle of women in Mrs. Brenda's living room, and we didn't need to ask why. It became increasingly evident that Papa God was talking to His daughters that night.

We slipped in as quietly as possible and joined in the prayers, worship, and intercession. I had been fasting all day to prepare myself to minister that night and had no other plan other than to love on the Lord and some precious women.

So it really was no surprise when Mrs. Brenda heard God change the plan for the evening and she called the younger two of my little group into the middle of the circle to pray over them. I mean, she HEARS and she OBEYS without question. I love that about her.

It was, again, no surprise that she called me to the middle to be with them...They're my bebbies, so OF COURSE I'm going to be with them!

Well, they got to prayin' and MAN! Those ladies unleashed HEAVEN on us, haha!

The girls were prophesied over and then…To my utter surprise...

Our precious...Very southern...Fearless leader, Mrs. Brenda, laid hands on ME and said, "You have EEEV-vry-thing you need to lead these young people! DO not be AFRAID! You have living WATER in your BELLAAY! You have everything you need inside of you to do POW-ER-FUL things and the fire of GOD…"

Well...I don't remember a lot of what else was said after that because at that moment someone blew a shofar over me and into me and...

Y'all.

I was a mess.

My insides were shaking.

FIRST off. I had said NOTHING to this woman about my personal struggle with teaching this series because of the total dependency I must have on my own ability to let Papa's love and compassion for healing flow through me with confidence. I know many of you don't believe that I struggle with confidence at times, but I really do. Especially when I am solely responsible for teaching these teenagers how to receive words of knowledge for healing...And how to heal people in general....When I feel SO inadequate.

I mean, at that point? I had had ZERO success in healing ANYONE (Yes...I tried...ALOT) or in getting ANY accurate words of knowledge since the Randy Clark conference I attended in February…How could I possibly DO this?? And how could she possibly KNOW that?!

I'll tell you how.

My Papa ratted me out, that's how.

I'm so glad He did. :)

Who? ME?! Yes, You...

So we are doing a series with our students this month...And to say that I am nervous and feel UBER under-qualified to even DO the stuff we are talking about, let alone TEACH it is...Well...The understatement of the year.

You would THINK that after the craziness that had happened at home group the night before, I would be FULL of confidence...BUT!

I wasn't.

(GASP!) I know, right?

I even sent Mrs. Brenda a text earlier that day asking her to pray for me and, God-love-that-woman, she zapped me (in love) and reminded me of a few things, lol.

Later Wednesday afternoon, the studhubs said he felt strongly that Papa was saying that before we started getting into the depth of this week's topic, that we should have a time of repentance and heart checking...To basically start the service backwards.

Which was so cool because, the songs Papa had given to me

for worship weren't the normal "pre talk" stuff. They were mellow and moving...Like 'decision time' stuff.

So that's exactly what we did.

What follows is a poor description of a few things that our mighty God showed us that night:

As a result of Shane's obedience to start the service backwards (LOVE that man!!), many students surrendered their unforgiveness and bitterness and laid their hearts open before God as the two precious little lambs, who were leading the worship that night, lost themselves in the spontaneous and in their own prophetic songs over their peers. It was a beautiful thing that is beginning to happen on a more and more regular basis now.

Then we got into the teaching.

O_o.

We talked about hearing God and learning how to recognize His voice, and then they got to practice it. After a few minutes of prayerful silence and instructions to raise their hand if they heard something, I went to a few who were willing to share what they had heard.

The things Papa said to them ranged from encouragement, to comfort, to gentle correction and eyes were wide all over the room, lol. I could almost hear the startled thoughts of different students all over the room.

"Did God just really talk to ME?? "

Yeah. It was pretty cute, lol.

Anticipation and faith were rising.

Then we moved into the deeper, more nerve-wracking topic.

(Gulp)

Words of Knowledge....What is it? How you get one? What does it look like, feel like...? Why do we get them sometimes? How does it relate to healing?

So with heart pounding, nervously, I jumped into the teaching portion of the topic...Excited, but to be completely HONEST? I was almost...Kinda dreading the next part...

The activation.

What if no one got a word of knowledge and we just...Sat there?

What if I didn't get one....?

(Bigger gulp)

I looked at Shane behind the sound booth...Maybe HE should come finish the next part....

I shook myself internally.

You STOP that!! Mrs. Brenda said you had all you needed inside to do this...And even more than her saying it...Abba, YOU said I would do this.

I was so scared...But God had said that I alone was to teach this...

So! I told them (in blind faith) we would sit quietly and the

Lord WOULD give them a word of knowledge and for them to begin to listen...If they felt, saw, heard, or thought ANYTHING out of the ordinary to come to the front.

We sat for what seemed like forever.

I was shaking inside.

"Papa..." I watched the students with their bowed heads...Looking for evidence of His moving, like I had been trained to do. "Papa..." I was almost pleading, "if You don't do this, it won't be done... and what will happen to their faith?"

A few more painful moments went by.

And then…

One by one students began to make eye contact with me. Confidence began to trickle into my spirit. He was speaking.

I called them forward one at a time.

The first one said that their right knee had started hurting under the kneecap and behind the knee.

So I turned and asked the small crowd of students if there was anyone whose right knee was giving them trouble… Nothing....Annnnnd........Nothing.....Annnnnd...

Nothing.

HORROR!

No one moved and no one said a word.

Suddenly, I wasn't so concerned about my own failures, but my heart ached for the student who had so bravely come forward to share the word of knowledge...

"Papa..."

I had told them, earlier in the teaching, that sometimes we hear or feel things in the natural and its easy to confuse it with a word of knowledge, so we NEVER say that we are ABSOLUTELY certain, but that we also don't discount it. We speak it out making sure that the people know that we are not certain of it. If no one responds then, it's totally ok.

I was preparing myself to give that reminder and send an embarrassed student back to their seat, when I heard the Lord say,

"Ask again."

I smiled.

So I did.

And a timid hand slowly slipped into the air.

It was a new student. New to our house and new to the charismatic movement...

I asked her to stand, verified her condition and then simply said, "Holy Spirit, thank you that you have healed her knee."

"Ok." I continued with a very convincing confidence that I was not ENTIRELY feeling quite yet. "Now do what you couldn't do before without pain."

"Like...Now?" she asked uncertainly.

I nodded and smiled, "Yes."

She squatted a couple times and smiled...

...And I cried.

There were gasps all over the room. She had been healed.

We thanked God LOUDLY, haha, and blessed what Holy Spirit was doing.

She was the first of many as more and more students came forward and shared their words of knowledge and everyone who shared their word had one or more people stand across the room and all physical ailments that were presented were healed that night.

Even psychological issues were healed! Panic, Anxiety, Social Anxiety, Depression, Unforgiveness that had led to severe stomach issues...

GLORY TO THE LAMB!!!

He is able and willing and YOU CAN HEAR HIM. Listen for His voice and don't dismiss a passing feeling or notion...You may just be housing someone's miracle.

If I can do it?? If these students can do it?? So can you. HA!

WOOHOOO!!!

A TIDALL WAAAAVE IS COOOOMINNNNNG!!!!

The Harvest Unleashed.   WOOT!!

DO IT ABBA!!!

Y'all, I'm done. DONE. HA!

MOCKERY!!!

Let me start by saying that I have been the brunt of MOCKERY since October.

Jes kiddin'.

It's not really mockery. They just giggle when it happens, lol.

I used to do the same.

I would watch "the Frizzness" on Bethel's YouTube channel and would giggle when Papa would touch her and she would jump or twitch.

I giggled, that is, until it happened to me.

I was at a women's retreat and, well, He just dumped a TON of His glory right on top of me and I was a jumpy, twitching, uncontrollable mess. For a week afterward, I had a hard time talking about Him or TO Him without twitching so hard that I couldn't speak.

Thank GOODness I can talk about Him now with only mild jolts that are unnoticeable to anyone else, but they are little reminders of how very much He loves me and how very near He is to me...

Although...When He agrees with a statement I make or when He draws very near to me, haha, He will touch me and my whole body will jerk once or twice...Sometimes accompanied by an uncontrollable, "HEY!" or "WHOA!"

No matter where I am, or who I am around...

Try explaining THAT one away at the counter at the drug store, lol.

(TWITCH) "HEY!........How ARE ya??....GOSH! it's such an AMAZING day!"

Or

(JOLT) "WHOA!.....That's a GREAT deal!....Yeeeeah."

Hahaha!

The students would do the same thing...Laugh…Giggle...Think its funny or cute...

Lol.

I warned them.

What's that I see...??

Looks like some jumpy, twitchy teenagers to me...

Verbiage you might hear in worship and prayer around Encounter services, these days?

"Did you just twitch??"

(No Answer)

"You just twitched."

"Leave me alone. So did you."

And I LOVE it. Hahahaha!

Who's laughing NOW? HA!

Jes Cawl Me "Pearl".

I've been a little off lately.

A little quiet.

A little snappy at times.

A lot thoughtful and reflective.

A little...hermit-ish.

Noise gets on my nerves...Which makes navigating my day with six kids an adventure.

o_O

I just want to be left alone these days.

Crazy, huh?

To love people so much and yet just want to be away from people...

In the stillness.

In the quiet.

Alone with Him.

In our garden...Just the two of us.

Complexity frustrates me, when it used to not bother me one iota, and I find myself asking the question, "Why is this so hard?...I mean really...It's not that hard." And I take a deep breath and "ooosahhhhh" my way through practices, conversations, daily activities, etc.

I relish simplicity and solitude.

So, when I got an email from a prophetic community that I subscribe to and it spoke of simplicity, all of that kinda made more sense.

It spoke of how the Father was calling us to this place where less is more and more is less. This certainly explains why I feel the uncontrollable urge to simplify everything in my life...And by association, my family's lives get simplified too, haha!

Poor Family.

Even my worship has become more simple.

Now, I don't mean that I've become the one that just walks away from complex issues or turns their back on things and opportunities just because its not simple or convenient...Hang out in my life for a week...HA! You will see it's just the opposite.

I mean that in worship:

I simply love Him.

   I simply adore Him.

      I simply talk to Him.

         I simply pour out my devotion on Him.

            I simply approach Him.

            I simply honor Him.

               I simply prepare to encounter Him.

Simply Simple.

So, the simplicity urge was explained...But I just couldn't put my finger on the "obscurity" and wanting to withdraw from public eye and recognition.

Even a new friend said, last night, that it was that lack of desire to be seen that caused Papa to trust me and put me in the public eye, and that I better get used to it...But I just don't want it right now.

Make sense?

Hear my heart. I want EVERYTHING that my Papa has for me, when He has it for me. If He says, "Go to that platform and release your gifts." I will put aside my aversion to the spotlight and go, happily...Joyfully...Knowing that my obedience blesses Him greatly.

 I love Him, so I go with no resentment or insecurity. I simply mean that, if I had my "ruthers", I would push someone else into that place instead of me...Not because I feel inadequate, but because I genuinely have no desire to be exalted. Hasn't always been the case, but it's where I am now.

...And I keep hearing the word,

"Obscurity"

Before I share the revelation that wrecked me today, I must rewind a bit.

I have a sister.

Not biological, but my sister, none-the-less.

We are spiritual twinsies. We are connected so deeply that even though she lives states away, we know when the other is struggling and we know when the other is praying...Among other very...Strange...Things, haha.

We are both POWERFUL prophetic worshipers in our own rites, but when we get together...Woah.

Holy Wrecking Ball, Batman.

So she came to Georgia, yesterday, and joined me on stage for an Encounter service. Needless to say, The Lion of Judah came in like a flood and swept us all away...Like He usually does when we worship together.

She had to go home this morning.

Sad Face.

Suddenly, I was struck with an insecurity I have not felt in AGES.

Our students have experienced **HER** worship, and they have experienced **MY** worship, but never have they experienced what happened last night when we joined our anointings and entered in as one...Together...In perfect unity.

Imperfectly Perfect.

The enemy of my soul whispered into my ear,

"You can not worship alone. You cannot worship effectively without her. You cannot go to those deep, deep places without her. The students loved your unified worship. If you lead them alone, they will remember this night and wish that she was with you."

Like I said, a LIE.

Normally, I can recognize it and call it what it is, but coupled with the fact that I know we are designed to worship together and that we most definitely will worship in nations together...And that I was SORELY missing her...And...

BAM!

Open door for the lie.

I texted her immediately and here is that text:

"Annnnnnd I just came under attack! Wow. I just got hit with STUPIDness. Ugh! It's a lie, but wow. I just had

this intense insecurity come over me that I CAN'T lead worship without you...especially for our youth...bc they have experienced our connection and it won't be nearly as powerful by myself! What in the world?! I REBUKE that! I am enough! I am powerful! I am His mouthpiece..."

And this is where is gets revelatory.

Who knew that an auto correct would lead me into revelation and holy wreckage..???

Haha..He did.

"...I am His mouthpiece and **hand made jewelry for the display of His splendor"**

Yeah. It was supposed to read "hand maiden".

It was right then that I heard the voice of my Papa God say,

"You are my pearl...The one I found in a field...The field I sold everything for and purchased so I could have that prize."

"Wait, what? A pearl...In a field..?? I have a field..."

My revelation sensors began tingling...Because, I have a field. It's our garden, mine and His and I go there a lot...This field of wheat...And He said I was a pearl that He found...And that He gave everything to PURCHASE the field that I was ALREADY IN and...

I could feel Him smile,

"You are a pearl...Made from a grain of sand...Cultivated in secret...In obscurity. I have kept you hidden to retain your purity and now I will put you with others like you in a strand to present to my precious bride

*as a wedding gift and you will adorn her neck with simplicity, purity,
and beauty at the wedding of the Lamb."*

OhdearGod.

I'm a mess.

I'm a pearl.

SHANDAI!

Holy Spirit…a.k.a. Legit Hind Parts Kicker

Run. He said to run.

So I ran.

No so far the first time, and He was mostly quiet.

But the more I was obedient to His command, the more chatty He became. The more He took on the role of physical trainer.

The more He began to show me the correlation between my physical actions and what was happening…or would happen…In the spiritual.

Take last night for instance:

I was pooped…And sore…

See, two days before, my eight year old daughter had this amazing idea that it would be 'fun' to do yoga together…Just us two…Mother and daughter.

First of all, yoga is not now...Nor ever WILL be fun.

Ever.

So like I was saying, mother and daughter yoga.

…Yeah..

That didn't happen.

Little stinker pooped out on me FIVE MINUTES into it and laid in the floor on her yoga mat, giggling at the unnatural contortions I was forcing my screaming body into.

X_x

SO!

Entywho. Fast forward.

I was NOT feeling the run last night, but He said to run, so I ran.

He warmed me up with a few stretches and some power walking and then we got into the work out.

"Okay, Holy Spirit, what are doing tonight?"

"*Run*", came the answer.

"Okay, I'll run." And I picked up the speed to a decent pace and ran...And ran...And ran...

And He was silent.

"Oh...Kay...Pa..Pa...When…Can...I...Slow...Down..?", I

panted.

"Not yet."

"Okay."

And I ran.

And He was silent.

And I ran.

And He was silent.

And I ran.

My lungs were on fire and even with my training in controlling my breathing, it was getting pretty tight in there.

At this point, in training with a human, one could rationalize reasons to quit...i.e. :

"They don't know my asthmatic history...so this could actually be dangerous for me."

Or

"They don't know that I can't breathe right now..."

Or

"If I pretend to pass out RIGHT HERE, I could totally catch

a few breaths before I get discovered and get my butt kicked again."

But HOW do you rationalize that stuff with the One who created your body and knows it better than you do??

You're exactly right.

You can't.

That nagging little epiphany hit me pretty hard right at that moment, and so I pressed on, no excuses.

As soon as that decision was made in my mind, I heard Him.

"Good! You can do it! Keep going! You're almost there! You've got this, girl!"

MAN! It was like steak and taters after a fast to hear Him encourage me like that. I was so tired. So incredibly tired. It had been a LOONNNNNNG day and all I REALLY want to do was go home and curl up with my java, my studhubs, and my Bible...But I didn't.

"Know what?? I CAN do this!" I set my face like flint (probably looked more like a grimace) and pushed on until I heard Him whisper,

"...and coast."

I slowed to a slow jog and then a fast walk.

"You must trust Me to lead you and set your pace. I know you intricately, what you can handle, what is too much and what is not enough. I also know when you are to arrive on specific platforms. Your

timely arrival depends solely upon your willingness to hear Me and run when I say run, and in your stamina to run as long as I tell you to run. You don't have to hear Me telling you what to do with every step, child. Just run. I see your struggle and your determination and when you feel like giving up, I will believe in you to finish. I will encourage you to finish. Will you believe in you? Will you heed the encouragement? Will you finish?"

I soaked that in.

So many things He is teaching me with this running thing...

Pace affects arrival as does endurance to maintain that pace.

Wow...Do I believe in me?

Wow.

"Now sprint."

I was kind of expecting that, so I chuckled and took a deep breath and "girded up my loins" and took off.

Honestly I was expecting to do longer sprints and had JUST stretched out my gait as I passed a streetlight and He said,

"Coast."

"Well, ok then." I slowed to a jog.

I was waiting for Him to drop some revelational nugget in my spirit as He has been prone to do during our training times recently, but....Nope.

I passed the next street light.

"Sprint."

And I took off.

"Coast."

And I jogged.

We repeated this quite a few more times and in the distance I could see two men jogging on the track a head of me. The more times He had me sprinting, the closer and closer I got to them. I was praying that I wouldn't have to sprint past them...Oh dear GOD how awful would THAT be?? 2 years of lazy flopping and shaking at high speeds past these two runners...Who looked like they knew what they were doing...

O_O

Just...No.

But of course, just as we (Holy Spirit and I) were jogging about 10 feet from them, the dreaded word came:

"Sprint."

Inwardly, I whimpered. After so many sprints on these out-of-shape legs o'mine...My poor hams were jelly and in that moment, I had a choice. I could continue to jog past them at a decent pace...Like I had never heard that hateful word, breathing hard but not struggling, to a 'safer' distance and then start my sprint...

OR

I could throw it into high gear, right there, and leave those two intruders dazed and confused in my jiggly, huffing-puffing, and COMPLETELY undignified dust.

I bit the bullet, swallowed my pride, and hefted this self into high speed. I ran a little farther than He said to run and my breathing technique went right out the window...Y'all, I wanted some DISTANCE between me and that humiliation.

"You have to be ok with running your race in front of others."

Still a little foggy from lack of oxygen and over-exertion, I didn't quite understand what He meant, at first, and I interrupted Him.

"But I don't understand why it matters WHERE I sprint, as long as I sprint, Papa, why did I have to do that...? Run in front of them...That was embarrassing and uncomfortable for them to see me like that...I know I don't know them..." I ranted, somewhat put out with Him, "...But still! Why can't I just sprint where it's just you and me...?"

And then it struck me what He was actually saying.

"Ohhhh....." I was silent and let Him finish.

"You have to be ok with running your race in front of others...And you must go hard, with everything you have, spending yourself and pushing beyond your comfort...even your own ability. What you perceive as embarrassing and uncomfortable is motivational and life changing for others. Just run. There will be times when we will run alone...we will train alone...you will sprint for Me and Me alone, but Daughter, You will and must run in a public arena and it's not for pleasure. You MUST run as if their very lives depended on it...for they do. Just run."

I was silent and had slowed to a fast walk. We walked together in silence for a while...Me just soaking in His nearness and Him just loving me. After a bit He broke the silence,

"Why don't we pick up the pace a bit?"

I chuckled, "Okay."

And I picked up an easy pace and just coasted.

"This is easier now."

I smiled. Yes indeed it was. It was even...Dare-I-say-it?...Pleasant. This pace that, at first, had my lungs DYING, was now one I could keep up for a long time...And I was prepared to do it.

And then.

"Take off your glasses."

NOT what I was expecting.

"What?! Why?! I can't see if I do that!"

"Yes, you can. You can see enough to keep your course. Just take them off."

"Alright..." I, somewhat nervously, took off my glasses and folded them up into my palm and ran almost blind.

When I say blind, I mean,

This.
   Girl.
      Is.
         Blind.

He was right, though.

I could see the track...Just not clearly.

"I have shown you dimly what your path looks like, but you can not see your destination. I alone see that. You must trust MY eyes to guide you on your path. You do not have to see where it is you are going to run this race I have called you to run, but you do have to trust Me and run it anyway."

Woah.

Wow.

Papa God, I will run. I will run as long as You say to run. I will build my endurance and I will believe in myself. I will push myself beyond my natural limits whenEVER you say to do it...No matter WHO is watching. I will run blind. I will trust You.

I DO trust You.

I'm loving this season I'm in with Him. When I say that He is training me, it means SO much more...That word "training" just holds fathoms more depth than I ever knew it possibly could and I am so glad that I chose to be obedient, in spite of my laziness and complacency, that very first time that still small voice simply said,

"Run."

The Name of The Game Is Slayer...

"WYATT! DON'T SASSINATE ME!!"

"Okay."

(gun fire)

"WYATT!! I SAID DON'T SASSINATE ME!!!"

(no answer)

"You have ta let me sassinate YOU!"

"You have to earn your assassinations."

As I sit here, computer in lap...Working on a completely different thought...I hear this exchange between a very frustrated Nacho and his older brother, and I look up from my writing and watch them.

I see the almost desperate face of my six year old as he whole-heartedly petitions his brother not to "sassinate" him and I see the utter calm and resignation on the face of his older brother, who is unmoved by his pleas and unceremoniously "sassinates" him.

"WYATT!!! LET ME SASSINATE YOU!!" Nacho demands desperately, but unfortunately his brother is not feeling benevolent.

"No."

(Whining) "THAT'S WHY I WANT TO JUST PLAY BY MYSELF!"

As a mom, it's tempting to intervene on behalf of my little...To step in and force his brother to have mercy because he IS just a little and is severely outmatched.

You see they are in involved in a game called "Slayer". It's a match of wits and skill where they search various maps for each other and whoever has the most kills in a set time period, wins the match.

I watched and almost intervened when I heard Papa say:

"No."

So, now, I'm faced with the ever echoing, "Why?" and I begin to process what is unfolding in front of me.

Here is what I see:

1) A little boy who knowingly entered a match of skill and wit, full of confidence, with a much older, more skillful opponent.

2) A little boy who underestimated his own skill and the skill level of his opponent.

3) A little boy who becomes seriously frustrated and demands his opponent to allow him to "sassinate" him.

4) A little boy who decides that playing the game alone would be more beneficial to his mission...One that began to assonate the opponent and has now changed to roam a map alone, randomly blowing up unimportant props so he can feel like has accomplished something...Then after a bit he challenges his brother again....With the same end result.

5) An opponent unwilling to compromise or surrender...Because he knows he is the inevitable victor.

6) A desire to intervene.

And here is what Papa showed me:

1) How many times do we knowingly enter into a battle with our enemy, so full of confidence in our ability to take him down?

2) How many times have we, and do we, sorely underestimate his skill level versus our own?

3) How many times do we become frustrated and really wish he would just slow down so we could "sassinate" him and feel better about where we are spiritually?

4) How many times do we decide that, when we discover that we aren't as skilled as we thought we were, it's not worth it and we would be better off playing the game alone and change our mission to exclude real warfare and include a lot of explosions of irrelevant 'purposes'?

5) Our "opponent" is uncompromising and unwilling to surrender and just allow us to slaughter him...Because he knows we lack the knowledge of who we are.

6) Intervention only enables the victim mindset.

So, I dutifully I switch writing topics.

1) I can't even count how many times I, myself, have done this. You know what I'm talking about...That moment when you have been playing against lesser demons and you have emerged victorious from your battles, confident of your ability to conquer the next level up. We KNOWINGLY enter in to battles with enemies who outmatch us.

Now hear me. Death is defeated and Jesus is King. Hell knows it, but sometimes, we don't. We catch glimpses of our identity and instead of pressing in to discover more and more, to "level up" if you will, we take our finite knowledge of the kingdom and run with it...Straight into a match with a prince that exceeds our "skill level"...And because we are ten-foot-tall-and-bulletproof, we march right into...

2) Underestimation. Just because Jesus defeated Hell, doesn't mean that Hell responds to us in the same ways. Even the disciples got their hind-parts soundly kicked and Jesus had to handle it. It wasn't that they didn't have the power, it was that they didn't have the know how...Or the skill for that particular demon. They had done this before and they just assumed that this time would be just like the rest...But it wasn't. And....

3) OH. How. Frustrated. We. Get. We start throwing out desperate threats...Hoping that our words would somehow convince the enemy that we are really more educated and strategic and that it would allow us to gain the upper hand.

Our less than convincing 'rebukes' and extravagant quotations of the right "scriptures" sound much like my six year old's attempt to use the proper terminology to the enemy.

Comical and childish.

See, we have this misunderstanding that the kingdom of darkness doesn't know the Word as well as we do...But they have known it since the dawn of creation...For Jesus, Himself, is the Word. When we have a simple face knowledge of Jesus and His scriptures, but no heart knowledge...No revelation...We sound as helpless as we really are...Like little girls and boys trying to use big scary words that we have no idea what they mean or how to properly pronounce them.

Then we become confused and begin to question the power of the name of Jesus and our own ability to conquer darkness when we demand that we be allowed to "sassinate" and the enemy ignores us, openly defies us, or soundly whips us.

I saw another mental exchange happen with my two sons and this one really just...Wow.

Wyatt had assisted in the set up of a particular map and knew it like the back of his hand. He knew where the hiding places were and where the transports were. There were times when he strategized and allowed himself to be killed because he knew that where he would respawn would be beneficial to victory in that match.

Yep. Our enemy does that too. Lures us into a place of his design and deceives us into thinking that this 'kill' is the important one, and we go in guns blazing and eradicate the enemy only to have him respawn in an area that we never expected and he takes us out.

Wow. Looking back, I've been a victim of that on more than one occasion as I'm sure many of you have, as well.

4) So we get mad. Indignant. Discouraged. We get tired of being beaten at every turn and instead of learning from our mistakes or spending time learning how to win, we decide that it's easier and better for us to roam the map alone with no challenger, rationalizing that this will help us gain skill in our military tactics. And we run around making a lot of noise about what God has done and how He has used us in the past, but we avoid what He is doing NOW.

We fire upon things that have no relation to our purpose or destiny. Imaginary enemies...Things that have no threat or power...And we feel better about our artillery until, without ever having entered His presence to be trained, we enter into the same match we were defeated in earlier...With no more power...No more knowledge...And no more chance of beating him than Nacho has of beating his brother.

God, help us.

5) And our enemy meets us again. And we demand his surrender. And he laughs at us. Why would he surrender a battle he has already gained the upper hand in? We have no idea of the power we hold...Of the Kingdom authority we actually possess...And he knows it.

There is a devastating self-inflicted plague of kingdom illiteracy among the children of God and as long as the enemy can keep us in the repetitive circle of defeat and self-service, then he will never have to surrender the dominion that Jesus DIED to return to us.

Because that's what the battle is actually for: Dominion.

6) Then we ultimately get pretty ticked about why God does not intervene on our behalf...Why He seems to watch from a

distance while we suffer defeat after defeat in the same arena.

You know? My first child crawled early. He talked early. He walked early. When my second child was nine months old and he wasn't even crawling, I was concerned. The pediatrician assured me that he was neurologically normal and that he was just different that his brother...And sure enough, he started crawling in a few more weeks and then began walking shortly after.

Speech was another thing altogether. Again, the pediatrician assured me that he would speak soon enough and that I would miss the silent days. At two years old, when he only had about ten words, though, his pediatrician began to dig a little deeper into his development. At one appointment, he observed as Wyatt grunted and pointed to his cup and I responded by giving it to him. Then when he grunted and I couldn't make out what he wanted, Tucker (his elder by nineteen months) interpreted for him.

The pediatrician smiled and told me in no uncertain terms that I was the reason that Wyatt didn't speak. I was mortified and offended...But he was right. My son had no reason to learn to speak. I knew what he needed and gave it to him...And I was crippling his ability to communicate.

As I thought back on Wyatt's slower development, I realized that I snuggled him a lot (NOT a bad thing!) and the child was hardly ever on the floor. He was either in a swing or in my arms the majority of his infant life. He couldn't learn to crawl because I never gave him the opportunity to.

In the same way, if our Papa constantly intervenes in things for us, we will never learn to stand on our own. Never learn to operate in the power of the Spirit if we never have defeats that send us back into His presence to learn WHY we were defeated and HOW we can overcome it. In His great mercy,

He allows us the necessary defeats so that we may grow in our knowledge of Him and in who we are in Him...If we will resist the urge to play the game alone when we get discouraged.

This has me thinking and I wonder...

What would happen if we actually knew the Word?

What would happen if we actually knew the enemy's map as well he does?

What if we actually understood warfare and strategy?

What if we stopped expecting God to save us from our own laziness?

What if we actually knew what the weapons of our warfare REALLY were?

What if we actually spent time training with Him?

The name of the game is Slayer.

I think I'm ready to BE that...For real. Instead of an easy target. Actually...I'm pretty ok with being a Juggernaut. The one who is almost impossible to kill because of their camouflage, invisibility, and shields...The one the opponents are intimidated of and watch their backs because of.

Yeah. I like that.

"*I do, too.*" And He smiles.

Cheaters Never Prosper...Or Do They?

As I'm preparing for a word I'm to speak soon, and I'm studying through my talk relating to the previous chapter on "Slayer"... I hear:

"Cheat codes."

And it gets me to thinking.

Hmm...Cheat Codes.

Well, let's explore this a sec.

In relation to video games, Cheat codes are for those who want to advance quickly without having to actually learn the game...Without actually having to struggle through the battles. While it is CHEATING, and normally I would be adverse to skipping out on the process, I can see how this is beneficial.

Don't hate. You know at some point you have pulled out that owner's manual looking for a hint only to find just enough info to piss you off. Haha!

I mean

COME ON!!

Help a gamer out!! JEEZ!!

And! If you think about it....The writers of the games come up with these codes...Well...Writers and hackers, lol.

ANYWHO!!

So! For the sake of argument, let's assume that God is the writer of this game and that many of us are stuck on a certain level with a particular enemy that has us blocked.

We. Are. Stuck.

Like…STUCK - stuck.

So, in a stroke of genius, we refer to the manual....Only to find JUST enough info on how to basically maneuver the maps...So it causes a frustration in us that drives us to dig deeper until, at GLORIOUS last, we find the CHEAT CODES.

Using these codes we can easily conquer this enemy OR completely by-pass it altogether.

So, What IF:

What IF time is running out in this game and we only have a set amount of this precious time in which to defeat this foe to reach the destination and save the world.

What IF every second counts, and the enemy knows it?

What IF there are cheat codes that are available to those who are not ok with being stuck.

What IF we read the manual and it doesn't seem to give us enough information on the surface?

What IF we ask Holy Spirit to "counsel" us on how to read this manual effectively...?

What IF we have revelations?

What IF we test it out?

What IF, armed with this new info, we can easily defeat this foe?

What IF we can avoid this battle altogether?

What IF?

Hmm.. Food for thought.

Letting Go

*1*Oceans.

That song.

Dangerous to your faith...And your life.

Not too long ago, I read a blog post that circulated throughout a popular social media outlet that talked about not singing the lyrics to "Oceans" unless you meant it. For those who may be unfamiliar with it, here are the lyrics that will cause you great difficulty if actually taken to heart:

"OCEANS"
Matt Crocker, Joel Houston, Solomon Ligthelm
(c) Copyright 2012 Hillsong Music Publishing

VS
You called me out upon the waters
The great unknown, where feet may fail
And there, I find You in the mystery

In oceans deep, my faith will stand

CH
And I will call upon Your name
And keep my eyes above the waves
When oceans rise my soul will rest in Your embrace
For I am Yours and You are mine

VS
Your grace abounds in deepest waters
Your sovereign hand will be my guide
Where feet may fail and fear surrounds me
You've never failed and You won't start now

BRIDGE
Spirit lead me where my trust is without borders
Let me walk upon the waters where ever You would call me
Take me deeper than my feet could ever wander
And my faith will be made stronger in the presence of my Savior

 I was one of the many, I'm sure, that heartily "AMEN"-ed the post and joined the multitudes of passionate "lovers" on social media who thought of the many people who sang this song without realizing what it actually meant and applauded the author for actually saying it.

Today, I heard the song on internet radio...For the millionth time (insert eye-roll here). I'm just being real. I mean, there are only so many times you can hear a song you love before you get sick of it.

When I heard the first few measures of it, I almost changed the station...But I decided that I hadn't heard it in a while and, honestly, I was just getting settled after plopping the Bug down for a nap and I just didn't feel like reaching for the remote.

Wow. That sounds just as lazy as it is.

Ha! Oh well. It's true.

So any way, as I'm responding to some messages before I open up "Big Honkin"(My huge archaeological study bible), I feel my Papa draw ever so near and I hear Him whisper,

"Release..."

I inhaled His presence and thought of that particular blog.

Then I thought of something I never have before.

What about the people who are still in the boat watching their loved ones step out into impossible circumstances that make absolutely no sense and are just so impractical that it seems almost stupid and irresponsible.

What about those people?

I'm of the mind that, as hard as it can be, to be the one climbing out of the boat is so much easier than to be the one watching this process...Sometimes helplessly.

What happens when those we love so dearly hear the call of the One whom their souls love?

What happens when He says, "Come." and they respond by nervously, excitedly, or in great fear and trembling, stepping out onto the waves?

Are we willing to allow them to get out that boat...? Or do we disguise our lack of faith with talks of practicality, common sense, being responsible, and everything that could happen or go wrong? Do we shout encouragement or do we fill the atmosphere with doubt, unbelief, realism, and fear-based arguments creating the very storm of confusion that distracts them from the Hand that beckons to them?

Are we willing to let them run with Him on the waves...And are we willing to allow them to sink and let Jesus be the one to lift them?

Not judging, by any means...Just thinking. Lord knows, I'm having to learn this.

The disciples left perfectly good jobs to follow an unknown man and I'm pretty sure many considered that pretty irresponsible and risky.

Again, Just...Thinking.

Thinking about times when I've been on both sides of this scenario...The times when I was released...And the times when I was held back.

Thinking about the times (notice the plural) when I was so afraid of what COULD happen that I interfered in what God had planned for another's journey with Him.

Thinking about the season that my family has entered into, where we are both the ones stepping out and the ones watching the process.

I'm seeing that song, "Oceans", is just plain dangerous all around.

Those who are still in the boat have to mean it, too.

Sometimes, we have to be ok with letting someone jump into crazy, impossible, sometimes-senseless circumstances. We have to be ok with not giving fear a voice. We have to be ok with fervent prayer before we say a WORD...And we have to be ok with the fact that they just might sink...But that's Papa's concern. He loves them more than we do and He's such a good landing pad.

(Disclaimer: This is all based on the understanding that the person stepping out has actually spent time seeking His heart and has spent enough time with Him to know His voice)

We've got to let go...Even when it makes zero sense and it scares the bejeezus out of us.

I still hear Him say, *"Release."*, and I'm realizing it goes both ways.

The one leaving must release the comfort and safety of what life was "supposed" to look like...They must release their grip on their own destinies.

And the ones yet in the boat must release the one whose heart is to obey recklessly.

...And trust God.

...And the God in them.

...Because He is.

...And He's got them.

Ascending The Hill...

With A Bossy Dog

I sat outside, this morning, on my spiritual mom's patio with my Papa God waiting to hear from Him as to what He wants to speak to his kids this evening. He was quiet and so was I....Just enjoying our time together in the silence.

Words are overrated at times.

Sometimes we just need to BE with Him...

And thennnnn.....*Riley*.

See, my "mama" has this dog.

He's quite a character.

He's grumpy and a tad bossy, lol.

He's an opportunist. Do NOT leave your food close to the edge of the table...Or unattended.

PERIOD.

He's a sneak and he's completely adorable in all his spoiled-rottenness.

He's Riley.

And he taught me something.

On this morning, he insisted to come out with me, so I obliged him. (If you know Riley at all, you will know that, oblige or not, he tends to have his way, haha.)

I sat there, soaking in the cool morning breeze...Loving the embrace of my Father, and I noticed Riley doing a normal dog thing. He was running all around with his nose dragging the ground.

I assumed he was looking for a place to do his business, but nope. He was looking for a rock.

It wasn't long before he found the right one and brought it over and set it beside me on the metal patio chair. He sat down and looked at me. No wagging, no whining...

Just....Staring at me with these big, droopy, brown eyes.

At a loss for what he wanted me to do, I chuckled and said, "Well, thank you, Riley."

Serious butt-wagging happened and off he went.

This process happened several times...About six or eight is more accurate, lol, and with each new rock, he would line it up beside the last one and wait for the "Thank you, Riley!"

It was really quite impressive!

I mean he legit lined them up, and it really seemed that he needed to hear thank you before he would go get another.

Eventually, he finally stopped going to get them and sat there looking at me.

"Thank you, Riley!" Had no more effect.

So I got this bright idea to throw one.

Bingo. That's what he wanted all along, lol. Sneaky little thing. Here I was thinking he was being sweet and bringing me presents and he was just bringing me the tools to entertain him.

But isn't that how we are too?

Kindnesses with an agenda?

We will find those who we feel can give us what we need or want...Or maybe can get us somewhere...Or that their talents and gifts will benefit us...And we shower them with kindnesses and opportunities, but here is no honesty in it.

"Here! Have this (fill-in-the-blank)!"

And we wait for recognition.

Then we get bored with it and the real agenda begins to rear its ugly, manipulative head.

"Entertain me...I did this for you...Now you do this for me."

And when our "toy" gets wise and stops playing our game, we get grumpy and bossy...like Riley.

We will cover you and support you as long as:

      -you are doing what we want you to do
      -we can directly benefit from what you do
      -we can take credit or receive recognition for what you
          do or what we've done for you

But we will get pretty darn grumpy if:

      -you stop doing what we want and begin to do what
          SomeOne else says
      -people begin to see that we aren't really responsible for
          what you are doing
      -we can't duplicate what you are doing and people begin
          to notice

Heaven help us...Forgive us...

And still yet, our wonderful Father thrills in showing mercy
and mercy is victorious over judgment.

So if you find yourself in Riley 's position...Repent with your
whole heart and receive mercy.

And if you find yourself in the toy's position...Mercy triumphs
over judgment.

He loves, so we love.

He forgives, so we forgive.

He is unoffended, so we choose to remain unoffended.

I recently heard someone talking on the subject of
Stephen...He was so misrepresented...So misunderstood...So
not playing by their rules...And they were quite grumpy about
it and they stoned him.

The stoners laid their coats at the feet of a young man named Saul.

Stephen chose to see Jesus. He saw the Lamb of God standing at the right hand of God. He lifted his eyes beyond the eminent stones and boulders that would be hurled at him and he saw Jesus. And then he uttered some of the most powerful words...Words that mirrored very nearly what Jesus, himself, spoke.

"Then falling on his knees he cried out in a loud voice, 'Lord, do not hold this sin against them!".... *(Acts 7:60)*,

Wow.

What if...

What if the Damascus road experience for that young zealot named Saul...What if all the epistles and letters and miraculous signs and wonders....What if the radical way this entire world has been affected by that young zealot, could be traced back to the decision that Stephen made **to** remain unoffended...?

What if *"Lord, do not hold this sin against them..."* Led to *"Saul...Why are you persecuting Me?"* Led to *"I, Paul, an apostle of Jesus Christ..."* Led to *a jailer's salvation....*Led to *churches planted all over...*Led to *your salvation...My salvation...Our intimate knowledge of the love of God....?*

What if?

You know? I don't find more than a few references to Jesus actually standing at the right hand of God. I've heard more than a few preachers say that Jesus was standing because of Stephen's martyr...But...There were many, MANY martyrs.

People who were much more 'effective' if you go by exploits and time on earth.

So, what was so different about Stephen's martyr?

I can't say that this is the Lord...It's only my opinion, but I think it had to do with Stephen's completely unoffendable heart. In the moment of his greatest pain...He chose to let go...Not only of his own claim to justice, but he released the destinies of each and every one of those responsible for his death, to the Father.

And Jesus stood.

Not as an "attaboy", but out of great respect for the sacrifice...Not only of Stephen's life, but of his right to be offended.

Maybe you are dealing with an offended heart?

I offer you this simple prayer that has helped, and continues to help, me remain unoffended and pure in His sight and releases those who hurt me, betray me, misrepresent me, use me, disrespect me, attempt to stop what God is doing in and through me... and many more things, to be free to be all God intended them to be.

"Father, I bless them. Do not hold this against them. Have mercy upon them. Make all their wildest dreams come true. I bless their finances and their households. May they be fruitful And multiply. Bless their relationships. Father would you give them peace and sweet sleep at night. Bless their dreams. May they encounter You in new ways every day. I release them to be everything You designed them to be in the womb. Father, I love them because You are love and I forgive them because, You know, how much you have forgiven me for. I do not hold onto the lies that the enemy has spoken about them or over them. I will not come

into agreement with the dark agenda to destroy any area of their lives. I bless them! Now, You bless them indeed!!"

2"Bless those who persecute you; bless and do not curse." - Romans 12:14

One more thing.

I've been thinking a lot about the scripture*:*

3"Submit yourselves, then, to God. Resist the devil, and he will flee from you. Come near to God and he will come near to you. Wash your hands, you sinners, and purify your hearts, you double-minded. Grieve, mourn and wail. Change your laughter to mourning and your joy to gloom. Humble yourselves before the Lord, and he will lift you up."
James 4:7-9 NIV

 Wash your hands, it says.

Purify your hearts, it says.

It reminds me of another scripture:

4"Who may ascend the mountain of the Lord? Who may stand in his holy place? The one who has clean hands and a pure heart, who does not trust in an idol or swear by a false god. They will receive blessing from the Lord and vindication from God their Savior."
Psalm 24:3-5 NIV

A pure heart.

You know, Acts says that when they looked at Stephen, they saw the face of an angel...The face that mirrored the purity of his unoffended heart and it infuriated them.

Could it be that a pure heart is an unoffended heart?

Could it be that to choose to remain unoffended frustrates our enemy and causes him to flee from us?

I don't presume to know the answers for you, but my own personal experiences tell me, yes.

In my own life, the kingdom of darkness has no power over an unoffended heart that refuses to retaliate, but loves deeply and blesses those who persecute it.

Let's all ascend the mountain of the Lord together...The view is amazing

ENDNOTES:

1 – Acts 7:60 Holy Bible, New International Version®, NIV® Copyright © 1973, 1978, 1984, 2011 by Biblica, Inc.®

2 – Romans 12:14 Holy Bible, New International Version®, NIV® Copyright © 1973, 1978, 1984, 2011 by Biblica, Inc.®

3 – James 4:7-9 Holy Bible, New International Version®, NIV® Copyright © 1973, 1978, 1984, 2011 by Biblica, Inc.®

4 – Psalm 24:3-5 Holy Bible, New International Version®, NIV® Copyright © 1973, 1978, 1984, 2011 by Biblica, Inc.®

Resonance

The baby grand.

The single most desire of this little girl's grown up heart...And Jesus wants to give me one.

My love affair with the piano started when I was very young. My grandmother had a small one in her parlor and I remember closing myself into that room and playing random notes...Trying my hardest to mimic the sounds that I could hear so loudly echoing in my heart. When other parents would have told their child to stop, because it was most definitely NOT lovely, haha, they allowed me to explore the endless possibilities of musical combinations and sharps, flats, naturals and accidentals that a piano keyboard holds.

Unlike other a lot of other small children, I rarely banged the keys. It was more like...Oh, I don't know...An unspoken respect that I felt for that instrument and I played it with an almost reverence. It was full of mystery for me and I remember spending hours in that room...Just me and the sounds of exploration. There was a genuine sadness when we had to leave because I knew it would be months before I would be able to experience that again.

When I was ten years old, my family moved into a new home and the former owners had an upright piano. It was very old and heavy and they didn't want to move it, so they offered it to my parents at a reasonable price. My parents knew the love I had for this instrument and they accepted it and immediately signed me up for piano lessons with a dear friend from their former church.

I was almost delirious with happiness. It was a dream come true for me to have this beautiful, antique, cherry piece of living art just sitting in our living room waiting on me to caress its keys anytime I wanted to...Which was a lot. Haha. I sometimes wonder if the real reason that my parents signed me up for lessons was for their own sanity.

I was in love.

And then...

The day came for my first lesson and I was beside myself with excitement. I rounded the corner of her kitchen and stepped into the living room and laid my eyes, for the very first time, on the baby grand piano. I'm moved with emotion even now as I remember that moment. It was ebony and shiny....And the stuff dreams are made of.   The lid was down and had lace draped across it and their family photos were arranged symmetrically there. The keys were beautiful and so white and shiny compared to the yellow, antique ones on my own piano and when she beckoned me to sit beside her on the bench, it was with great awe and reverence that my ten-year-old self slid in beside her.

She motioned for me to touch the keys and she was speaking to me, but I didn't hear a word. I was lost in the moment of discovery and wonder. The keys were so smooth and cool and when I pressed down on one, there was a glorious resistance against my finger that my upright did not have. In that moment, I was forever smitten by this brilliant, glorious instrument and my practices at home were less about learning the material, technique, and theory but more about imagining what the perfected pieces would sound like on my teacher's baby grand.

Once a week, I was allowed the honor to sit on that bench and pour my heart into the instrument of my heart.

Time passed and my skill grew quickly and with acquired skill came the confidence and freedom to create. Haha! I remember times when I would sit down at the baby grand and play an assigned piece and my teacher would stop me and say, "Nicki...What's happening in the left hand? That's not what's written." To which I would reply, "It was boring, so I made up my own." Haha.

This became the norm for us. I would create and she would insist that I play what was written...Which was actually beautiful, now that I think about it. My teacher was very wise and the discipline has served me well.

One day, about 3 years in, I worked up the courage to ask my teacher to open the lid of the piano. I had only dreamed of what that would sound like. She smiled and I helped her move all of the pictures and the lace drape off of it. With great care, I helped her lift the heavy lid and set the prop in place. She showed me all of the strings and hammers and she had me stand beside it as she played for me.

It was almost more than my thirteen-year-old heart could bear. It was exquisite. I watched the hammers strike the strings and the sound was indescribable. I felt the vibrations of every note echoing through my body and as I closed my eyes, I inhaled the resonance...I took it into my heart, and in that moment I decided that if I ever had a dream in life, it would be to own one of these instruments that could literally change the air in the room with one solitary sustained note.

I opened my eyes and looked at my teacher. She, too, was lost in the bliss of that moment. Her eyes were closed and her body was moving in beautiful sync with the pianissimo and forte moments...Literally feeling each note as it escaped the confinement of her heart and exploded with purpose and melodic dignity into the atmosphere. If I had ever had a hero, in that moment, it was her. She understood...And I've rarely ever felt so known and understood as in that moment. We were connected by the passion we both shared for this stunning compilation of wood, metal, felt and strings that expressed our hearts so beautifully.

She finished her piece and just sat there...Eyes closed, soaking...As the resonance of the last chord slowly died into pregnant silence. There was a reverent hush and she opened her eyes and looked at me and smiled. "I think I might just leave it open..."

For the next 3 years, I played on the open baby grand until the day when my teacher sat beside me on the bench and said the words that I never wanted to hear. We had just finished a beautiful duet and she put her arm around my shoulders and said:

"Nicki...That was lovely...You have grown so much, physically (I was now 16) and musically...And there's nothing left that I can teach you. You know all of it and the only thing left is to continue to play and challenge yourself."

My lessons ended that day and it was the last day that I would touch a baby grand on a regular basis.

I grew up and married and my upright came with me many times, until it got to the point that it really was too old to continue to move. The sound plate, which holds the strings and maintains the tension, was cracked and it just needed a home where it could sit and never move again. With a heavy heart, I sold it and from then on had keyboards to accommodate our active life style.

I began to lead worship and keyboards were just so easy to transport...And while everyone else was experimenting with all of the cool synth sounds...I found myself gravitating to the grand piano sounds...And for years it was enough.

But then…

Recently, I pulled out my son's keyboard to play. It's how I pray. I played the first chord and I was just...Unsatisfied. I turned it up as loud as it would go. Still no connection. I put in ear buds. Nope. I found myself frustrated because I couldn't seem to get the sound I was looking for. I ended up turning it off and putting it away feeling unfulfilled and unsettled. The next day I wanted to play, so I pulled it out again and the same thing happened.

For a week this went on and I found myself just disgusted with the synthetic sound of the grand piano function. I cried out to Papa. "Papa! I'm longing for resonance....To be surrounded by palpable inspiration and beauty...I can't TAKE this synthetic anymore! I don't even want to TOUCH a keyboard because it's FAKE! It sounds JUST enough like a piano to suffice, but its missing the depth and complexity and REALISM. "

*(**DISCLAIMER** Please do not misinterpret. I am in NO WAY saying that keyboards are fake instruments or that keyboardists are fake musicians. Synth is an art and I have great respect for the brilliant musicians who create using that medium. I have personally played and still play amazing keyboards from amazing companies, but as a classically trained pianist, I am simply stating my longing for the sounds*

of original instrument and the revelations I have had.)

SO...In essence I threw a fit.

In that moment, He began to show me the beauty of resonance.

In many ways, the American church has become much like the keyboard. Good intentions and helpful hearts have lent a hand in making the gospel of Christ easier to manage. The weight of it has been lightened and many options have been added for diversity and creativity. What once was a pure sound has been synthesized and downsized to a sound that is very close to the original, but lacking one vital part....Natural resonance.

What creates this resonance? Tension. Pressure. Impact. Openness. All things that cannot be synthesized or imitated and when it is, it carries no weight.

When played alone, a decent keyboard (set to grand piano) sounds convincingly like a grand piano and can be moving when played skillfully. But when set side by side with the grand, there is simply no comparison. When a song is played on the grand...Especially an open one...One literally feels the music. There is an actual physical reaction that happens in the air. Frequencies are released that affect our bodies physically.

So it is with the gospel of Christ. We can simplify it. We can add cool sounds to it. We can downsize it to make it more acceptable and portable...But in doing so, we lose the natural beauty of it...And there is something majestic about knowing that His gospel is too heavy to move or carry in our own strength.

When one approaches a grand piano, one approaches with a sense of smallness...A sense of reverence...And when one sits at its keys, there is a sense of humility and appreciation of the honor that it is to partner with this instrument to create ripples in the atmosphere. Children are not left unattended with it because if its great worth and value. Novices feel unworthy to touch its keys...but yet there it sits...Unconditionally accepting us at any level of expertise and patiently waiting for someone to be bold enough to approach and play the song only tension, pressure, and impact can create.

Our lives are much the same.

Too many of us live our lives synthetically...Imitating a sound we have heard, but never truly experienced...Adding cool things to that sound to make it better or more attractive to others in the name of relevance....And we shrink back from tension and pressure of any kind. When our lives are impacted, because we avoid tension, the sound that is released...Instead of being a clear resounding note that grabs the heart of the listener, it becomes a dull, out of tune ear sore.

Pressure is also something we don't like, but if there is no pressure, no matter how tuned and tight the strings of our hearts may be, our convictions are not strong enough to create the necessary impact for the sound of freedom to be heard.

If we could ever truly experience the resonance of His love and a life lived in partnership with Him, our hearts would forever be gripped by the complex and stunningly simple beauty of the melodies created from tension, pressure, impact and openness, and we could never settle or be satisfied by a substitute no matter how convincing.

I think this is much of the issue with the way the world views believers. We have become synthetic...Constantly changing the sound we produce in a desperate attempt to relate to the changing world around us...When in reality? The world is simply looking for something real...Something pure...Something unchanging and constant...Something so secure in the impact is has on the world around it that it doesn't have to change...It doesn't have to move...It can just simply, and gloriously be.

He is still revealing so much to me in this area and, as He speaks, I soak...Dreaming of the day when His promise to me is fulfilled and I am once again seated at the cusp of discovery, surrounded by inspiration and the frequencies of exploration, joy, sorrow, longing, love, passion spiral like ribbons toward the heart of the One whom my soul loveth.

In a word: Resonance

Kitty Shenanigans

We have 2 new kittens… Süßi (pronounced "Zues-ēē) and her sister, Schatzi. They have no tails and are...OMGSH!!!! SO FRIKKIN CUTE!!!!

Being littermates and tail-less are the only things these two have in common, lol. Süßi is super sweet and a little shy and Schatzi is super sweet, sassy, and completely fearless.

And then there's Po...

Him's my fweet-punkin-smooshie-face-baby....Not a mean bone in his fluffy body until...

The twins arrived.

I have never heard him hiss or growl in his whole 18-month-old-life until the two little, no-tailed, kittens joined our family.

From the first moment he investigated their tiny, tail-less bodies, he decided, "Thanks, but no thanks" and proceeded to let them know that he was in NO WAY interested in their kitten shenanigans.

Süßi was easy to convince, being the shy and timid one...And she avoided all confrontation with Po at all costs. Schatzi, on the other hand, saw it as a challenge to befriend this hulking, hissing fluff ball with no nose. Every time I turned around, she was chasing him or getting too close for his comfort and he would slap her and hiss and run away.

Then he started purposely taking toys that the "girls" were playing with and he would hiss and growl if they tried to get them back. Süßi would watch him take it...Sit there contemplating for a minute...And then walk away to find another toy that he would eventually take away as well...Total jerk, lol.

Schatzi wasn't so easy to bully, haha. Po would snatch her toy and when he would look away, she would sneak back over and take it back. A chase would pursue and end up with a few hard slaps, a disoriented kitten and a toy that was left for Süßi to pick back up and walk away with...Only to have it taken away again...And you get the picture...Same scenario all day.

Two weeks have now passed and I was watching the three of them yesterday. Po and Schatzi have come to the understanding that he can't escape her and he has accepted her, and (gasp!) befriended her. They chase and wrestle and, yes, he still pops her hard but, dang it, she gives it right back.

 Süßi, on the other hand, is still unsure of him. She still cowers when he comes near and she will willingly leave a toy if he even looks at it. He knows this and, while he doesn't growl quite as much as before, he still pushes her out.

As I was thinking about them this morning before I started cleaning, I felt Papa saying that many of us are like Süßi...Timid and shy about things that seem impossible or bigger than our understanding. Schatzi enjoys access to relationships that are bigger than her because she was fearless in pushing her way into them. She's a little, squirt-of -a-thing but she doesn't know that. In HER mind, she's a lion. Because of this, she has been accepted into a 'higher' club.

You know? Schatzi and Süßi are sisters...But Süßi can't pull on that relationship to "get her in" with the older cats. It doesn't work that way. It's the same in higher levels of influence and life. We may get our foot in the door by who we know, but we won't be able to walk through that door and call it home unless we exhibit the same confidence and fearlessness as those who surround us.

Many of us long for higher "relationships"...Connections with people of influence that could greatly benefit us or catapult us into greater things, but we are like Süßi.: Happy to be included, but timid and shy and afraid to be assertive because, in our hearts, we don't really feel like we belong there.

What we don't realize is that the people and areas that we desire respect confidence and risk. Like Schatzi, it may not go very well at first. We may get slapped a few times...Hissed at...Growled at, but in time, our determination and integrity will earn the respect of one who will then make room for us at their table.

It's time for God's people to stop being so timid about our giftings, claiming a false humility. We were meant to influence the media, the government, the schools, the business world, the medical world, etc... We will never do this if we are shy little kittens who feel like they have to bow every time someone "bigger" than us growls.

Sometimes people of great influence will do this because they know that, to be a person of great influence and a catalyst for change, you can't bow to every person that hisses, growls, or slaps at you. You have to be able to stand your ground, with respect, and give back just as good as you get.

The last thing I noticed was that Schatzi never got angry or pissy with Po's treatment of her. She truly saw it for what it was: a challenge to know him more. Can we just stop getting so damn pissy and butt-hurt?! Don't let resistance and opposition offend you or discourage you! Stay in the game and stay unoffended! See it as an opportunity to investigate and see into the lives of others.

I work in film and it can be one of the most stressful jobs on the planet. I have been mocked, yelled at, cussed at and about, and yet I stand up for myself and give it right back. Know what?? I am still one of the most sought after in my market by productions. You want to know why?? Because I don't shrink from a challenge. I am confident in my ability and knowledge and, while they may rage on about whatever has them stretched to the max that day, I remain unoffended and I will give it back to them just as boldly, but with respect.. whether I get respect from them or not. I see them as people who have the world on their shoulders, instead of getting emotional and offended because they didn't honor me. This has earned me a place of respect in very high places and it has earned me access into the lives of people with great influence.

SO! I guess what I'm trying to say is: Stop being a cotton-headed-ninny-muggins about things seeming "impossible". Jump in and go for it...Even if you are the smallest little kitten in a room full of fluffy, pissy, hissing, big cats. You might just find a home there.

Ascending the Hill

Ascending the Hill

Storm Damage

Storm Damage.

I think video footage of massive storm damage is among the most heart-wrenching things to watch.

Video footage of people's lives, well-being, dreams, hopes....Just....Leveled.

It's been six years since a tornado ripped through our small town and the lives and hearts of many were permanently affected

Six years since hopes and dreams were crushed and life as many knew it changed forever.

Every day we drive past the scars...Although houses have been rebuilt and lives have slowly moved on, the land has yet to recover. Once majestic trees now stand as ghostly reminders that something terrible happened.

We pass one of the paths that the tornado took, everyday on the way to and from school...To and from town...To and from anywhere. At first, it was a solemn reminder of lives lost, a beacon of hope that humanity was not lost, and for our family, a grateful prayer was said every time we passed it for the sparing of our family and loved ones.

But as time has passed, it has become less and less of a memorial and has even become, dare I say, common place to go past this place without a thought...Even to the point of using the tornado damage as landmarks for giving directions...

"Turn left at the dead end, just past the tornado damage."

Or

"If you pass the tornado damage, you've gone too far."

The other day, I was driving past a particular area and I happened to glance over at the tree graveyard that used to be a densely wooded area. I saw the skeletons of trees, and new growth that was coming up and I remember thinking, "It sure is taking a long time for the land to heal..."

It was in that moment that the Holy One began a conversation with me.

I want to share it with you:

BEGIN DIALOGUE:

"It sure is taking a long time for the land to heal."

"*Yes, and it is sad.*"

I nodded. "Yes, Papa, it is. So much was lost that night. "

"Yes...There was much loss." He continued, *"Look again."*

I snatched a quick glance as I was passing the last of it.

"Can you see My Goodness?"

I smiled, because I could see it. New growth was happening all around and I knew that eventually, all that growth would over take the death and the scars, while still there, would be covered and hidden by life and beauty again.

I could feel His pleasure.

"This, Beloved, is how it should be...But sadly, with many of my children it is not."

I could feel my revelation sensors tingling. I waited for Him to continue.

"Terrible things happen. Sometimes evil, sometimes consequence, and sometimes simply because the world is fallen...and that" He referred to the storm damage, *"Is what is left behind in their lives."*

 I began to understand what He was implying.

So many times we experience life-altering events in our lives and our lives bear the scars of these events. Depending on the severity of the impact, people can look at our lives and see very clearly that something terrible has ripped our hopes, dreams, and future plans mercilessly apart. These events leave their effects behind for years, and years after the fact people can still tell that something traumatic has taken place.

What happens a lot of times is that we never allow ourselves to see the regeneration of promises, dreams and hopes after these events. We look at the scars and we see the death of our lives as we knew it. We see hopelessness. We see fear of the unknown.

We see the storm damage.

But all around our broken dreams and ripped hopes and hearts, the seeds that fell to the ground unnoticed in the good seasons, have taken root and are growing...Never to replace the lives we had before, but to create a new season of beauty all its own.

I have stood in a forest where trees have been ripped up and I have focused on those old and young trees that now stand as a dark reminder. I have also stood in that same forest and allowed my eyes to travel down, away from the gray and dead bark, to the vivid greens of the new life slowly creeping up around them. I have felt the sense of tragedy and despair, and I have also allowed myself to feel the hope of something new and beautiful growing out of such tragedy.

So if you have been touched by the hand of tragedy in any shape, form, or fashion, will you allow yourself to hope again? Will you allow yourself to breathe again? To turn your eyes from the grey and broken places and allow yourself to see the fragile seeds of hope rising all around you? Because they are there...If we choose to see.

The "Modifier"...Oh Good Lord, REALLY?!

I can't think of a better description for the last 5 weeks of my life other than...Complete hell.

Well, at first it was.

Now that I'm in a rhythm, it's actually getting to the point that I am remembering why I loved working out 5 years ago...But it took a minute, lol.

As I was dying the other day, I happened to look up at the screen of my computer where my workout for the day was in progress. I was sweating and grunting and almost crying from pushing through each round of torturous exercises and my eyes landed on "The Modifier".

You know that one....That one person in the group of

badasses who is a little fluffier than the rest. The one who does a different exercise than the rest and lifts different weights than the rest. The one that makes it ok to be complacent with your workout program and commitment to yourself.

I know, I know. They are there for those who, like me, were and are not at the fitness level to completely go all in with the exercises that are presented in each work out. At first, I was IN LOVE with "The Modifier" because she was fluffy like me and I could feel like I had worked out because I kept moving instead of stopping altogether...Sometimes...Lol.

But As I grew stronger and pushed myself to actually try the real exercises and as I felt the pain of that effort for days afterward, I began to resent "The Modifier".

Yesterday afternoon was an active recovery day for the program I am involved in. We did Pilates and, don't let anyone ever tell you that any mat class is easy. Lawd, no.

AnyWHO!

I was butt deep in leg raises and such and I happened to look at "The Modifier" and her "exercise". I was disgusted. I was like, "What the hell?" (I find myself cussing a lot in workouts…because, well…just because PAIN) "Is that even a leg raise?? What IS that?? Seriously?!" And then she was like, "Oh, I can feel the burn!"

"What?! You feel the burn? How do you feel the burn when you don't even have your leg lifted off the ground at all?? You're barely doing the move at all!! Just enough to say that you've done it."

I found myself yelling at the screen and venting to Shane as we were literally moaning through gritted teeth to finish that God-awful leg series. Lol. Poor man.

Then tonight, as I was forcing my triceps to do work with a heavier weight, the trainer on the DVD went to "The Modifier" to check her form. We were pumping our heavy weights with both arms simultaneously while "The Modifier" was "pumping" one arm at a time with weights that were lighter than the 'light-weights' I began the program with. I never noticed this before...And tonight? Well, It pissed me off.

When "The Modifier" made the statement, "You gotta do the work!" and "Oh, I'm feelin' it!" and "I'm definitely gonna feel this tomorrow!" I was mortified at the hypocrisy and stopped mid-pump and yelled at the screen...As if she could hear me.

"You're gonna feel it tomorrow?! You have, what? TWO POUNDS and you are doing ONE arm at a FREAKING TIME! You aren't even feeling it NOW!!"

Shane was like, "Haha, Nicki...You have to let this go..."

To which I shot him a look that said, "Tell me you don't agree that this is ridiculous...", huffed and heaved my weights back into motion as my weary triceps screamed until the interval was finished...Rolling my eyes every time the trainer mentioned "The Modifier."

Please hear me. I totally get the modifier. I'm not bashing the idea of "The Modifier"...IDK, maybe I am? ANYWHO. This person is there for those who have physical restraints and I know that some people get discouraged. Having the token, fluffy exercise-cheater on screen helps to keep people from quitting, but honestly, I think that this is a lot of our problem in this culture.

Even from the beginning of the program I'm doing, I tried to actually do the REAL exercises and after a few reps, would drop back to what "The Modifier" was doing. I was heavier than I have been in my life and was SO out of shape. I couldn't reach my toes in a sitting stretch...Not because I was so tight, but because my stomach was in the way. I was thankful for "The Modifier" because she helped me feel ok about not pushing myself. If the real work began to burn too much, I knew I had an escape and I could still say that I had worked out.

Some where around week 2.5 or 3, I was like...Why am I not seeing the results like this program claims?? I'm following the meal plan, like a freaking Nazi...I'm doing the workouts every stinking day...

Then one day, the trainer said, "If you want something you've never had, you have to do something you've never done."

It sparked something and I began to process. I've had a tight, healthy body before. I know what it takes...Then one of the people working out on the DVD said, "There's no magic pill." To which the trainer agreed and said, "You gotta do the work."

Then I listened as she introduced a man who was killing himself with high-knees and she asked him how much weight he had lost since the few weeks he had been on her program, to which he replied between gasps "Thirty" gasp "Five" gasp "Pounds!"

He was sweating and working so hard, and here I was "modifying".

Ouch.

It was then that I realized that "modification" is not always beneficial.

Then Papa started talking to me about "Modifying".

I love when He challenges me.

How many of us look for "The Modifier" in our lives from the very beginning? We get motivated to take steps in a certain direction and then we see what it will actually take and then, "NOPE!" We tell ourselves we can't DO that, and we settle for a lesser form of what it truly takes to get the results we desire. Then, we are confused and frustrated as to why we aren't progressing as fast as we should be, if at all.

I remember a time about a year ago, when I started a different program but didn't have the meal plan to go with it. I have done this before...Like I used to actually be a trainer of sorts, so I assumed that I knew all I needed to know and could do it without the actual plan. YeeeahhhhhNO.

Two weeks in to having my hind parts soundly kicked with ZERO results...Like AT. ALL. I was like, "Bump this.", and I quit.

One thing my trainer says is that you have to do the work physically AND do the work in the kitchen. It takes discipline in BOTH areas to see results. Some people do the work and can't say no in the kitchen and some are super disciplined with what they eat and barely do the workouts. It takes discipline to say no to chocolate...Especially when one (Who shall remain unnamed...COUGH...me...) is PMS-ing and has vivid dreams of relishing a big...Glorious...Velvety...Piece of chocolate cake....All crumbled up and mixed in with homemade vanilla ice cream...(SELF! NO! STOP!)

It takes discipline to schedule in a thirty minute butt-kick when you've worked all day, done homework until supper, haven't seen the kids all day and they are crawling and climbing all over you with a thousand questions that all begin with "Mama!", and you haven't had a moment to breathe...Sometimes we have worked out at 11:30pm and midnight, simply because being consistent is not innate...It's a decision...And a rarity, these days, I'm convinced.

I said all of that to say this: Consistency and initiative are somehow being lost in this generation...A generation where we get trophies because we tried and where we have an escape if an exercise is too difficult. Where we rationalize "cheat days" and applaud those who don't finish.

Ouch...Did I just say that out loud?? Lol, I'm feeling a little sassy tonight!

In Hebrews 12:1 it says, *1"Therefore, since we have so great a cloud of witnesses surrounding us, let us also lay aside every encumbrance and the sin which so easily entangles us, and let us run with endurance the race that is set before us,"*

You know? When I first started this program, I REFUSED to let anyone workout with me or even be in the room with me. Why? Because I was mortally embarrassed, that's why!! It was ugly. I couldn't breathe, I was out of shape, and all my juicy flopping e'rwhere??

 No. Thank. YOU.

Nuh-uh.
I didn't want any one to witness that mess...ANNNND, if I'm being honest? I would've had to work harder with an audience...And I flat out didn't want judgment or feeling like I had to perform. There was zero accountability. I could "modify" all I wanted and no one would know.

But you know? The writer of Hebrews has a way of slapping that laziness right outta fool. "Hey, You! Since you are surrounded by a ton of people watching you, why don't we just drop the facade and get our tales in gear and stick with this thing...All the way through. No modifying or quitting allowed. " The NHV (Nicki Harris Version, for those who don't know, HA!)

Run with endurance. This verse haunted me. I wasn't doing anything with endurance by doing the easy thing. I wasn't building endurance. My trainer said, "Strength doesn't come from doing what you can already do. Strength comes from doing what you couldn't do before."

It finally clicked and it was then that I began to push myself every session to do more, to lift more, to hang in longer, to push my body beyond what my mind said it could do and believe in the machine that it was created to be.

I worked, and I worked hard. Instead of starting with "The Modifier", I started with the real exercise. I pushed my muscles to failure and when they did, THEN and ONLY then did I drop back to "The Modifier"...But only for a few seconds and then right back to it, I went. I found myself getting stronger, able to go longer, able to lift more and ultimately losing weight.

In life, we MUST start with the end in mind. Paul says in 1 Corinthians 9:24-27:

2"Do you not know that those who run in a race all run, but only one receives the prize? Run in such a way that you may win. Everyone who competes in the games exercises self-control in all things They then do it to receive a perishable wreath, but we an imperishable. Therefore I run in such a way, as not without aim; I box in such a way, as not beating the air; but I discipline my body and make it my slave, so that, after I have preached to others, I myself will not be disqualified."

We MUST operate with discipline and tenacity. We MUST push ourselves beyond what we are comfortable with...Beyond what we feel we are capable of if we are to be taken seriously as individuals and as believers.

I look at the American church and I see a fat, lazy, bride who is waiting for someone to motivate her into motion...Constantly modifying...Seeing just enough results to satisfy, and claiming that she is something she is not...Which is healthy.   I also see a turn in the tide. I see a generation of those who are rising up and refusing to accept a lazy gospel.

Those who have seen its powerless, toxic effects, and have determined that there is a race to run and souls to be won. Those who have decided that modification is not beneficial and have begun to do something they've never done before...To grow and trust that they can do what Jesus said they could do in John 14:12. Those who will do this until they fail and then get up and do it more, knowing that with every failure, more strength comes. Those who refuse to settle with "Just Enough". Those who refuse to be known as "The Modifier."

You know? I'm kinda done with being the cookie-cutter, sweet , pristine example of what a "Christian" is "supposed" to be. I think that's one "modification" that I'm saying good-bye to. It's exhausting and makes me COMPLETELY irrelevant to the culture that I work in and the people that I do life with. I cuss a little, when the point I'm making needs emphasis, and I'm just done with religious ka-ka. (See? I didn't cuss just then, when I could've said shit...oops.)

SO! Run, guys. Run hard and fast. I'm running with you.

PS. I think we care more about some things than Jesus ever did or does.

PSS. I love Scuppernong wine...Thank you, Jesus, that it counts as a fruit in my meal plan. You really do love me.

PSSS. I have discovered that I have no sympathy or patience with people...Women especially...Who tell me that they can't change their lives. Yes, you can. If THIS juicy can do it, so can you. Stop being lazy and quit yer whining.

Ok. Think I've made enough enemies, shocked enough grannies, and exhausted my rant...Maybe I can workout now and NOT yell at the screen...Until the ab workout and then, so help me, I can't be responsible for what comes out of my mouth when I see "The Modifier" in THAT one. Jesus help.

That is NOT a flutter kick.

ENDNOTES:

1 – Hebrews 12:1 Holy Bible, New International Version®, NIV® Copyright © 1973, 1978, 1984, 2011 by Biblica, Inc.®
2 – 1 Corinthians 9:24-27 Holy Bible, New International Version®, NIV® Copyright © 1973, 1978, 1984, 2011 by Biblica, Inc.®

Mom, Mom, Mum, Mum, Mommy...Shoot Me Now.

Today, I'm thinking about this afternoon when I'll be trapped in the car with my kids who have been cooped up in a classroom all day with no permission to speak freely.

I'm thinking about how many times I will hear "Momma!" or "Mommy?" or "Mom, Look...Mom!"

And can I be honest? My skin starts to crawl a little. From the time I get the first child in the car at 2:30pm to the time we get home after picking up the Senior from Cross Country practice at 4:00pm, I will have been fielding non-stop "Mom!" questions for a solid hour and a half...With no break.

See, I have 5 kids at home now, so when one inquisitive mind is satisfied, another thinks of something they want to know...And most times, they are so lost in their own quest for the ultimate knowledge that they demand my attention before I'm even done answering the first one....I need coffee...or wine...Just thinking about it is giving this hermit-ish mama anxiety...

Its so bad, some days, that I just can not take another,

"Mom!" and I will say, with hard-fought-for control and fleeting patience:

"No more, "Mama"! I'm not "Mama" anymore. Do not call me that again...Be creative and think of another name to call me. I will answer to the one I think is most creative....ANYTHING but "Mama" or any derivative of "Mama". "

I have been "Purple Pansy".

I have been "Coffee Turtle".

I have been "Daisy Petunia".

I have been "Puppy Farter".

Hey...It works, haha.

So I'm thinking about all this and then this pretty amazing question pops into my noggin:

"Papa...is that why You have so many names??"

I could feel His laughter echo through my Spirit.

We sat comfortably, chuckling every few seconds together about the images that were running though my mind. I love time like this with Him. He let the moment linger a little longer and then He asked me,

"Do you know all of My names?"

I was thoughtful for a moment.

"No. I don't. I know you by the names that I have called upon...But I don't know all of them...Some are kinda hard to say, honestly, haha."

"Would you like to know Me a little better?"

I'm still sitting with this question.

Would I like to know Him better? Well, duh.

But I know that His invitations are multi-faceted. I know that to know Him as something means that we walk through the experiences to gain that revelation of His identity.

I do want to know Him better and my heart is wrapped up in the fact that He invites me to this...I love Him so...But fear is a real thing. I've been through so much...I don't know if I want to know the circumstances that will lead me to the knowledge of Him in every identity...But something draws me...

Like a magnet and a moth to a flame...It's almost irresistible...

Like, even though it means the laying down of my comforts and security...I kinda DO want to know Him better. I want to trust Him more. I want to love Him well. In my experience, when He has beckoned me in such ways, it has been hard as hell and I've lost relationships and truth has illuminated deceptions in my own mind and in the hearts of others. I've wept for days and weeks over betrayals and realization that I was believing men and leadership...Honoring them instead of honoring God...But at the end of it, He has always given me much more than I lost...Opened doors to understanding and revelation, and He's always been enough through it all.

So, yeah, Papa.

Maybe I do want to know you better.

I think I might put the internet to good use researching who You are instead of being mindless because my brain is over-stimulated on a regular basis.

God, help me. I think I really am going to do this.

I apologize in advance for any rants that come as a result of my intention to find out just Who He is in every arena of life.

Here we GO!

First Identity to discover: Jehovah Tsidkenu

How the hell do you even PRONOUNCE that?!

Pain is Weakness Leaving the Body...Errmm...Can I Just Stay Weak??

Hahahaha!

Y'all. I was working out last week and I went down for a "Surrender" and just about surrendered for REAL. This is why I'm always in the FRONT when I work out with my TV or my computer...So people who work out with me only see the back of my head and not the "Oh sh$#, I can't get up!" face. HAHA! Too much real, right here. Hahaha!

Ok. And we're moving on…

So, about six weeks ago, I started reclaiming my life and my health. I had my eating plan all mapped out and I was so motivated through the first workout. I weighed more than I ever have in my life and my health was scary. I'm asthmatic and diabetes runs in my family and I was well on my way to heart issues. My first workout in 2 years was an ugly one, but I completed it...Even if I did cheat a little.

It felt SO good to be active...Until.

About twenty minutes after I had finished the work out, my entire body began to get this tingly-numb feeling...My muscles felt like they were going to sleep and, from past experience in the fitness world, I knew this was an evil foreboding of what was to come...(shudder)

By the time bedtime rolled around, every single muscle in my body was tightening up...But not sore...Yet. All night, I was awakened by these tight muscles reminding me of the abuse I had submitted them to. By morning, I was exhausted from little sleep and I cannot begin to tell you the amount of pain that encased my body like a vice.

I tried to sit up, like normal, and nope. Hot fire shot through my neck, shoulders, lats, and abs.

"Sweet Lord...What have I done...? I can't MOVE!"

Momentary irrational freak out.

"Roll over...I can roll..." I reasoned with myself.

Gingerly, I attempted rolling onto my side to roll myself off the bed. No success. The slow approach wasn't working...SO! With a colossal grunt, I heaved myself onto my side and successfully landed myself, with a yelp and a thud, into the floor. Apparently the side of my bed was against me and moved about six inches inward during the process.

Cursed memory foam.

I found myself in a pile in the floor and there was no way to remedy this situation without using this pitiful pile of body that was vehemently protesting every movement. I placed my arms strategically, heaved myself onto my hands and knees, unable to control the yelps and cries coming from somewhere deep within, and clung desperately to the side table and the bed to pull myself onto my legs and then to standing.

I stood there sweating, electric shocks rippled through every part of my body and I wondered how the hell I was supposed to function?!

Cue the spawn.

My bedroom door burst open and the two littlest come bounding in.

"Mama! What's for breakfast?!

"Mama! Can I pick?!" (They take turns choosing shows on a streaming service we use)

"Mama! I didn't pee on myself!"

"Mama! Malachi woke me up...And I didn't want him to."

"Mama! Lily took my book..."

"That was MY book! You took it from me!!...Mama, doesn't Malachi need his medicine??"

Lol...Bless. I guess she had had enough of his exuberant, argumentative, energetic, triggered self...

I stood there and stared at these little monsters that think I hung the moon and it occurred to me that I had to actually adult in this condition.

"Sweet Lamb of God."

They looked at me in momentary confusion and then trailed after me as I stiffly moved into the bathroom. They hung with me, never missing a beat, while I moaned and leaned over the sink to spit out toothpaste. They tried to follow me as I made my way into what I call the 'toilet closet'. They sat outside the closed door, firing question after question as I pressed my hands against the walls, walking myself down in a effort to lower myself onto the toilet without actually using my legs.

And the fitness peeps say, "PREACH!"

Once down there, I was struck by the bleak realization that I had to get back up...And I decided that I was camping on the john all day.

"Mama?" a small voice came under the door. I could see the shadow of a little head...

"Yes, baby."

"Are you okay? I'm hungry..."

Big sigh. "Yes, baby. I'm coming out, now..."

Life doesn't stop just because I don't want to move....Oooh. That'll preach.

ENTYWHO.

You know? Most times, as long as you keep moving, the pain seems to ease a little...Most times...

It wasn't that way for me, this time. It was horrible....And the worst part?? I HAD TO WORK OUT AGAIN THAT DAY!

HORROR!

How is this POSSIBLE?!

I don't know if it was strength from heaven or just outright stubbornness and determination, but I worked out. It was UGLY, but I worked out...And I was in TWICE as much pain the next morning.

This was my experience the entire first week and by the end of the week, I think my body was actually in shock...Like for real. I had cold chills and was physically sick to my stomach. I popped ibuprofen during the day in order to function with some trace of normalcy, and in order to sleep at night, I took one of my son's low dose pain pills.

I remember thinking, "This is ridiculous. I don't remember EVER feeling like this...Please, God...Let this get better...I can't live like this..."

I know, I know...That was a wimp's cry, but Y'ALL! I was sho-nuff HURTIN'.

Then during yoga day...Praise the LAMB for yoga day...A memory from about 5 years before flitted across my mind.

Back then I was addicted to working out and being healthy, so I did many programs. In one of them, the trainer said something that was my mantra that keep me going when I wanted to give up..

As I was stretching pissed off muscles, Papa reminded me of this quote:

"Pain is just weakness leaving the body."

"Well, I must be pretty damn weak, Papa! This is torture!!"

"Shhhh, Beloved...Breathe and sink deeper...Deeper into the stretch and deeper into Me..."

With every twinge, tingle, and deeper stretch that almost took my breath, I would repeat..."Pain is weakness leaving my body..."

Then He began to show me the similarities between the body of Christ and my own body.

Our bodies are made prophetically...Meaning that we not only mirror our Creator, but we are a physical representation...Even manifestation of the Bride of Christ. A visual aid, if you will.

We become complacent and lazy, as a body, and we become susceptible to the issues of past generations. It's easier to lie back and drink a bottle than it is to actually prepare a nutritious, healthy meal that will nourish and sustain us. Proverbs talks about this...And the writer is pretty harsh.

1"A sluggard buries his hand in the dish; he will not even bring it back to his mouth!" - Prov 19:24

That is the epitome of laziness...But then...Isn't drinking a bottle of baby formula when you are an adult just as lazy?

Can't you just see that??

I can. The mental imagery is hilarious and ludicrous, yet if this is so unacceptable in the physical, why do we coddle and enable this laziness in the spiritual?

If this were to happen in the natural, the mental stability of that person would be drawn into question and they would be evaluated and placed in therapy to help them move from that state of mind into another. Why is it that, when this behavior manifests in the body of Christ, we pamper and coddle people...We refill their bottles with the elementary truths? When they receive something a little more meaty...Something that actually requires action on their part...Actually requires them to work their muscles in new ways, leading to soreness...They buck and throw a fit...Like spoiled babies and we cater to every whine and whimper.

Sadly...Many babies find themselves in leadership positions and we end up with a house full of brats who have no idea how to walk, nor do they have the strength.

Hebrews says in 5:11 - 14, 2"We have much to say about this, but it is hard to explain because you are slow to learn. In fact, thought by this time, you ought to be teachers, you need someone to teach you the elementary truths of God's word all over again. You need milk, not solid food! Anyone who lives on milk, being still an infant, IS NOT AQUAINTED WITH THE TEACHING ABOUT RIGHTEOUSNESS. But solid food is for the mature, who BY CONSTANT USE have TRAINED THEMSELVES to distinguish good from evil."

I didn't like the change in my meal plan. Hated it actually. I love carbs. Pasta, bread, potatoes...YES, PLEASE! I love fats. Cheese, BUTTER, real...Full-of-fat...Yogurt. I love sugar...And chocolate. BUT! I knew and I know that, if I want to change my life and my health, I have to change my intake. I need food that requires thought and preparation. I was used to just responding to my hunger with anything that sounded good...Anything that I could shove down in a few bites to satisfy the hunger.

We do that spiritually. We feed our souls what is convenient instead of what is healthy. If it takes more than five minutes, we are like, "Nah...Just give me the five minute 'Please and Thank You' and I'm good."

The lovely gift of hunger that He gave us is appeased for the moment and we can feel like we have fed our spirits and done our duty.

The thing that I'm noticing is that our bodies are machines. They are really phenomenal, actually. But even the most advanced machinery needs to be maintained for longevity. I can see such a huge difference in the way my "machine" runs, even after just six weeks. I don't get tired as much. My feet and ankles are not swelling. I can breathe easier. My thoughts are clearer. My emotions are more regulated. I have ENERGY.

The same goes for what we feed our spirits. Eventually, the human body needs more than formula. As we grow, our bodies require more protein and fiber and vitamins and minerals in order to function and grow properly, without defect. Why, then, are we ok with staying on formula?

I think it has a lot to do with laziness. It's easy to go to church and sit on a pew or in a chair and listen to someone teach. We want our pastors to tell us what to do, to put a propeller on our backs and wind us up and send us off. We run out of steam and then come back for them to repeat the process. But guys...This isn't even close to biblical.

Paul told Timothy to [3]"fan into flame the gift of God within you..."(Read all of this...2 Timothy 1:3-7) He goes on to say that we've not been given a spirit of fear, but of power, love, and self discipline.

Funny thing about self discipline...It means literally to discipline YOURSELF. It's not the job of your accountability partner, not your pastor, not your spouse...Jes you. You, wonderful, you.

The last part of Hebrews 5:14 really just slams the hell out of rationalizing complacency. "...who by constant use have trained themselves..."

Excuse me? Who trained who? They trained themselves.

I recently had a person contact me in regard to "helping you to achieve your fitness goals." While I understand this line of thought, it bugged me. Lady, I am my own worst nightmare. I am a crazy woman about my meal plan and a drill sergeant about my workouts. I am diligent because I don't want the hell that I'm putting my body through to be for nothing. I have a desired outcome and I'm the only one who can get me there, and I'm willing to pay the price everyday...Because it means that much to me.

Once I got through that God AWFUL first week, my muscles began to adjust to the punishment. I began to settle in and actually enjoy the work outs and then my trainer said this, "If at any point this begins to feel easy for you, that's when you push harder and increase your weight. That's where your results are."

UGH. What if I don't WANT to?? What if I LIKE enjoying the work out...What if I LIKE being able to move without serious backlash from pissed off muscles?? What if I just modify...

What if I never reach my goals because I was too lazy to push myself? What if I never progress past where I am because I'm ok with good enough? What if I never fully achieve what I set out to accomplish because I don't want to be uncomfortable...And sometimes in excruciating pain? What if I never see the fullness of God in my life because I'm unwilling to discipline myself and I depend on others to feed me? What if I spend my life weak and infantile, resenting those around me who have chosen to discipline themselves and move into the mature arenas while I'm left fussing in my crib, demanding attention?

Pain is weakness leaving the body.

Every day I'm growing stronger and the absence of muscular pain means that I need to push a little harder. Muscles that aren't used become useless...I look around and see a lot of "Love" muscles that need some working out...But that's just an observation.

Pain is weakness leaving the body.

Sometimes pain is a sign that something is very wrong...And sometimes pain is a sign that something is very right.

ENDNOTES:

1 – Proverbs 19:24 Holy Bible, New International Version®, NIV® Copyright © 1973, 1978, 1984, 2011 by Biblica, Inc.®

2 – Hebrews 5:11 – 14 Holy Bible, New International Version®, NIV® Copyright © 1973, 1978, 1984, 2011 by Biblica, Inc.®

3 – 2 Timothy 1:3-7 Holy Bible, New International Version®, NIV® Copyright © 1973, 1978, 1984, 2011 by Biblica, Inc.®

ABOUT THE AUTHOR

Nicki Harris lives in Milner, Georgia with her husband of 21 years and six children. She is a worship leader, songwriter, musician, children's book author, and she and her family are missionaries to Europe. Her passion is to see hearts healed and set free through the tangible embrace of Papa God.